RAISED
FROM THE
DEAD

by

FRANK TURNER

The Personal Testimony of
America's First Evangelical Anchorman

AuthorHouse™
1663 Liberty Drive, Suite 200
Bloomington, IN 47403
www.authorhouse.com
Phone: 1-800-839-8640

First published by AuthorHouse 4/10/2009

ISBN: 978-1-4389-4415-9 (sc)
ISBN: 978-1-4389-4416-6 (hc)

Printed in the United States of America
Bloomington, Indiana

This book is printed on acid-free paper.

Dedication

This book is dedicated to the Lord Jesus Christ
and
to Allyson (Ally), Rachel, Andrea & Austin
and
to the air that I breathe,
my wife,
Nicky.

RAISED
FROM THE
DEAD

by

FRANK TURNER

The Personal Testimony of
America's First Evangelical Anchorman

authorHOUSE®

Contents

1. The End of the Beginning...11

2. The High Life..29

3. A Moment of Truth..69

4. The Beginning of the End.......................................79

5. A Certain Man is Sick..111

6. You Talkin' to Me?..133

7. Only the Truth is Funny.......................................149

8. Raised from the Dead...169

9. What It Means to be Born Again............................229

10. America's First Evangelical Anchorman..................249

As I was being immersed in the baptismal pool; in that brief moment that I was being held under the water, thirty-three years of pain and heartache...anxiety and depression...twenty-five years of drug and alcohol addiction including twenty-two years helplessly and hopelessly addicted to smoking pure cocaine suddenly and miraculously...

CHAPTER ONE

THE END OF THE BEGINNING

For all his days *are* sorrowful, and his work
burdensome; even in the night his heart takes no rest.
This also is vanity (Ecclesiastes 2:23).

The Bible doesn't record what illness was plaguing Lazarus, the man in Bethany whom the Lord Jesus Christ raised from the dead, but the sickness that surrounded and shrouded Frank Turner goes like this:

Night after night I reported from the field, and anchored from the news desk. To a metropolitan Detroit television audience of millions I appeared affable, jovial, capable, and professional.

I had worked my way from the weekend to the weeknights and from the small-time to the big show. I'd won coveted awards including an Emmy and earned professional respect and recognition.

I had a high profile and a big paycheck. I drove an expensive convertible and lived in an exclusive high-rise. My closet was stocked with suits of every cut and every fabric in every color. I had racks of expensive shoes and could match hundreds of ties with hundreds of dress shirts.

Nightly access to the television airwaves gave me power and influence and the ability to earn the respect and admiration of strangers who considered me family.

I got hugs and kisses from mothers and grandmothers at the grocery store, the finest tables at restaurants without reservations and warm smiles and waves from people whose cars I passed in traffic.

I flew in first class to take lavish and expensive vacations at exclusive resorts. I ate what I pleased, drank what I wanted, consumed and indulged my every desire; but none of that worked. I couldn't become the person that having and doing all those things would seem to represent.

The plain and simple truth is that I was just *damaged*. If I had to give the sickness a name, I'd just call it damaged. I'd been dropped right out of the box and I needed to be fixed.

I was usually envied or pitied; encouraged or chastised. I was advised to pull myself together or suck it up and move on.

What I needed was to be fixed. I was broken, beat up, in disrepair. *Damaged*.

I'd never gotten past being abandoned and orphaned, I'd never gotten over being abused, raped and molested as a child, and I'd never broken free of being trapped in addiction.

> I'd never gotten over being abused, raped, and molested as a child.

And so eventually I was reduced to the man whose reflection I saw at the bottom of a full-length mirror one night in the bedroom of my apartment. It was a night spent like so many countless others. I was on my knees, one hand tightly gripping the glass pipe I'd been holding for hours, perhaps even days.

It was very easy and common to lose track of time in the haze of smoking pure cocaine. You might glance up at the clock and read 1:05 and then after what seemed like a few minutes look again and see 1:15; except before it was 1:05 a.m. and now its 1:15 p.m. and perhaps even on a different day.

Anyway, there I was on my knees trying to balance on my elbow, so I could maintain my tight-fisted grip on that pipe while the fingers on my other hand carefully combed the fibers of my plush carpet hoping to turn up the little chunk of rock cocaine that I was almost sure I had dropped earlier that day; or yesterday or whenever.

I had been holed up in that room for five or six days without food, without water, without rest and without ceasing to suck down the pure narcotic poison of cooked cocaine through that little glass pipe that I was gripping like a priceless jewel.

As I came around the corner of my bed in search of that little chunk, which if found would represent the last of what had been destroying my lungs, heart and brain for the previous six days, I caught a glimpse of myself at the bottom of that full-length mirror.

And while I focused my gaze, what I saw made me begin to weep. There I was, Channel 7's Frank Turner: rich, powerful, envied, respected and admired——reduced to my knees and staring at an image my mind couldn't fathom.

My eyes were sunken into their eye wells and ringed by black circles. My skin had a grayish pallor and was coated with

Frank Turner reporting live from the Democratic National Convention in Chicago, 1996.

the fine residue of cocaine that had been floating in the air and sweated through my pores.

Often that residue was so pure I could scrape it off my skin with my fingernails, flick it back into the pipe and smoke it again.

My eyebrows and mustache were thickly caked and crusted with even more residue that had been too much for my lungs to absorb and had been exhaled with each subsequent hit from the pipe.

Mucus that had built up to protect my membranes from the intense heat of the flame required to melt the cocaine and turn it to smoke had mixed with the residue and formed a light gray "goo" that was dripping from my nose.

My lips were dry, cracked and bleeding from days without water and irritated from the corrosive effect of the pure cocaine residue which had built up at the corners of my mouth and was burning the tender skin.

A shudder that started at my shoulders soon began to shake my entire body. I sobbed and my body heaved, but I had no tears. I absolutely could not believe my eyes. I had been in this mess more times than I could count and yet this was the first time I had actually seen it.

As I labored to my feet, the glass pipe still held firmly in my tightened grasp, my attention was diverted by the mass of pornographic images from the dozens of magazines spread across my bed.

Having been sexualized by force at such an early age

had imbedded in my brain a deep hunger and obsession for the strongest pornographic images. The effect of the cocaine only served to magnify and intensify that obsession.

Because I couldn't risk exploring these repressed sexual desires with anyone in person due to my notoriety and because the temptation to explore the desires was connected to the illegal drug use; pornographic magazines and anonymous phone sex became the outlets for exploring the illicit desires of my molestation-induced fantasies.

> I gave up and decided that I just wanted to die.

Taking in the whole picture all at once, of what my life, my mind and my desires had been reduced to was horribly shocking, frightening, disgusting and as traumatizing as any previous mental, emotional or physical injury which had led to it.

It was in that moment that I gave up and decided that I just wanted to die.

Love Child

Behold, I was brought forth in iniquity,
And in sin my mother conceived me
(Psalm 51:5).

I can't imagine the look on his face or the pain in his heart or the deep, gnawing, gut-wrenching lurch that took place in what must have seemed like the bottomless pit of his stomach when my mother Opratee told her husband Frank Turner that she was pregnant with me.

It was not an announcement confirming the gift of God to a loving marriage, or an announcement that warranted joy, laughter and the grandest of celebrations. It was the confession of an unfaithful wife confirming her adultery, a confession that warranted anger, tears and the harshest rejection.

He took the news like a man but what kind of man—I don't know. I never got to meet the man who looked his wife in the eyes after receiving that news and said, "Have the baby."

I never got to meet the father who glanced down toward the belly that was soon to swell with the child of another man and declared, "He will be *my* child." I never got to meet the husband who looked into the future of a fatherhood forced upon him by an unfaithful woman and told her, "You are still my wife."

What kind of man does that? A man desperately in love I guess, and so I always assumed that Frank Turner was a man in love with his wife. I have no real idea; it's just what I've always liked to believe.

He could have condemned me to death; but instead he chose to offer me life. He could have cast my mother with me in her belly, into the street; but instead he chose to give us the covering of his love and care. He could have abandoned me and called me a bastard; but instead he adopted me as a son and called me Frank Edward Turner Jr.

I don't know if Frank Turner Sr. trusted Christ for his salvation, but it's clear that God used him to demonstrate the love and sacrifice of Christ.

When God could've condemned mankind to death, He chose to offer us life through the sacrifice of Christ. When He could have abandoned us in our sin He chose to give us the covering of His love and care through Christ. And when He could've left us as bastards, He chose instead to adopt us through the shed blood of Christ and give us His name.

I don't know what Frank Turner Sr. believed, but I believe he did for me what God has done for us.

Six weeks after I was born, Frank Turner Sr. died.

And so this is how my life began: conceived in the womb of an adulterous wife, loved in the broken heart of a betrayed husband and born into a family that was already damaged by deceit and jealousy and about to be destroyed by heartache and death.

May I Be Frank?

People are so obsessed with living their own lives, doing their own thing, exercising rights over their own bodies, making their own decisions, following their own feelings and doing what suits them that they usually fail to take one important factor into consideration: they can't keep the consequences they cause and the damage they do limited to themselves.

When it comes to "living one's own life," one person's right usually becomes another person's injury.

My life began as a result of my mother having a "right" to

Above: Frank Sr. and Opratee celebrate their wedding.

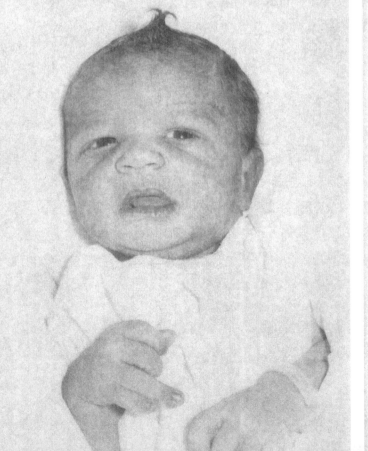

Left: Frank as a newborn.

live hers. She just wanted to "live her own life." But in living it through her adulterous affair with a man who was just "living his life," they *created* mine.

They passed on a generational curse to me, that before it was broken, caused a lifetime of death and destruction at my hands.

I'm a consequence they couldn't control; damage they couldn't contain. Not one of them actually *wanted* me to be conceived; not my father, not my mother and certainly not my mother's husband.

> Most of my life I didn't know *anyone* who actually *wanted* me.

No one wanted me but God. And for most of my life, I didn't know Him. So for most of my life I didn't know *anyone* who actually *wanted* me to be here.

Of course when I was a child, I didn't understand any of this. And so without any context, without any background, without any of the maturity of perspective that might help someone to digest all that was transpiring, all I could do was take each day as it came and wait to see what would happen next.

<hr />

I was born with the face of my father, Oscar Green and given the name of my mother's husband, Frank Turner. Six weeks after seeing his name joined with the face of the man his wife used to betray him, Frank Turner died.

My father by adoption was dead; my father by the flesh was gone. I had missed them both. Another consequence they couldn't control; more damage they couldn't contain.

I don't know what was going on in my mother's mind. I've only imagined and assumed it was shame and guilt. What I know for sure is that she drank heavily, ate excessively, smoked fiendishly and disappeared frequently.

Often she was gone for days at a time or longer, with no indication of whether she would ever return or if she was even alive.

Four months after I turned six years old, she died. After years of abandonment, my sisters and I had been orphaned. *Another consequence…and more damage.*

I ended up alone and in the care of my maternal grandmother, Lynne Johnson. She was an evil, vicious, and emotionally disturbed woman who had actually been in love with Frank Turner Sr.

She was jealous over Frank's love for her daughter, resentful over her daughter's betrayal of Frank and particularly distressed over the prospect of spending her golden years raising

Left and below: Little Frank

the bastard child of her daughter's indiscretion.

I had the name of the man she loved and the face of the man she hated. I was a daily reminder of all she felt cheated out of and all she was suddenly burdened with.

>
> I had the name of the man she loved and the face of the man she hated.

Lynne turned my life into a living hell of physical, emotional and verbal abuse that included almost daily lashings with her tongue and beatings with whatever kind of weapon she could put her hands on. *Another consequence…and more damage.*

For reasons known only to her, Lynne never protected me from the molesters she knew were victimizing me, and on at least one very long and painful occasion when I was about eight years old, even facilitated my rape and sodomizing at the hands of two of her male acquaintances.

During what seemed like an endless road trip from Chicago to San Francisco and then on to Portland Oregon, she knew that while one of them was driving, the other was in the backseat with me.

During every meal and bathroom stop she knew that while one of them was at the table the other was in the restroom with me. Every night, she knew that whichever one of them was not in her room was in my room with me.

Above: Frank as a boy.

Bottom left, center and below: Frank's grandmother, Lynne Johnson.

Sexual abuse is a particularly evil crime that somehow twists the mind of the victim into believing he or she is actually responsible. It leaves a feeling of filthiness in your flesh and scars of sadness on your soul. Being raped makes your heart heavy and your emotions weak.

> Sexual molestation does damage for which no words can describe.

Sexual molestation causes consequences and does damage for which no words are adequate to describe.

CHAPTER TWO

THE HIGH LIFE

Why do You stand afar off, O LORD? *Why* do You
hide in times of trouble? (Psalm 10:1).

The whole concept of taking or using anything to get "high" was unknown to me until I actually did it. As strange as it may sound from a former drug addict, there was a time when I didn't understand that people drank and smoked; snorted and injected stuff to alter their mental state.

I was aware of drunkenness but not that drunkenness was the actual aim of drinking. I thought being drunk was simply an unfortunate side effect of having *accidentally* had too much to drink.

Like anyone else, I was aware of drugs and that people used and abused drugs, both pharmaceutical and illegal, but I had no reference with which to understand the *purpose* behind it.

I didn't realize that people, *more than anything, wanted* to get "high," "hammered," "trashed," "stoned," "wasted," "messed up," and "laid out."

I remember one of my uncles drinking beer in my home soon after my mother died. At six years old, I had no idea what beer actually was. But it looked so golden, so sparkly, so cold and refreshing.

When my mother was around, she had prided herself on being the consummate hostess and had often thrown lavish parties, so of course she had the perfect assortment of glasses for every cocktail including beer glasses.

My uncle used to pour his beer into the tall slender curved glass, tapered at the bottom, just like it was done in the beer commercials.

I would watch the sparkling golden liquid run down along the inside of the slightly tilted glass, pooling at the bottom and beginning to form just a hint of foam. Then as the glass filled, he would tilt it straight up and pour the last couple of ounces from the can as he lifted it high above the rim of the glass, the last splashing drops of beer helping to form a head of foam to the glass' rim.

Wow.

I had no idea what it tasted like but I thought it sure *looked* good. One day after realizing that his little beer pouring ritual had my rapt attention, my uncle asked if I would like to take a sip. I couldn't wait!

The golden foamy beverage had sparkling little bubbles still floating up from the bottom of the glass. The ice cold beer was already causing the glass to sweat and tiny drops of water were running down the outside of the glass, cutting little paths through the condensation that was forming. It *really* looked good!

My uncle handed me the glass and with great anticipation

I pressed it to my lips and took in a mouthful.

It was awful!

I couldn't decide whether to swallow or spit it out and while trying to do both at the same time I coughed and sent half of it up my nose! I choked and spit and my eyes watered and my throat burned and the bitter taste coated my tongue while the foul alcohol smell filled my nostrils.

I absolutely hated it.

I couldn't understand how something that looked so good could taste so bad. My uncle laughed out loud and almost dropped his glass as I handed it back to him. He said beer wasn't for children, but one day when I got older I would develop a "taste" for it.

Mr. Turner's Neighborhood

My neighborhood, in which I had spent my entire life to that point, was in transition. The Hyde Park area of Chicago on the city's near south side was bounded on the south by the sprawling campus of the University of Chicago and its medical centers.

On the north, there was a grand display of elegant and historic mansions. On the east, there was Lake Michigan with its expensive and luxurious lakefront high rise apartments and condominiums.

And on the west, modest and low rent apartments and kitchenettes could be found all the way to Cottage Grove Avenue which was the barrier separating Hyde Park from the encroachment of distinctly more dangerous and poverty-stricken neighborhoods.

In fact, except on the east side where premium prices of lakefront property and Lake Michigan itself protected residents from change, there were dangerous and struggling neighborhoods encroaching on Hyde Park from every direction.

Some of the neighborhoods had fallen victim to the riotous and violent demonstrations of arson and looting in response to the assassination of Dr. Martin Luther King Jr. in 1968. Others had simply suffered as a result of unemployment, street gangs, crime and drugs—the usual suspects.

I grew up in an area that was tucked right in the middle of Hyde Park. It was marked by tasteful and elegant brick townhouses, and large apartment buildings of either red or brown brick that occupied entire city blocks and featured sprawling six and seven room flats.

As a little boy, before the neighborhood and my life changed completely, I lived in a richly textured, beautifully decorated apartment in a red brick, four-story building that had twenty-seven units and was originally owned by my father, Frank Sr.

Like so many other residential dinosaurs, it still stands today taking up nearly half the block in each direction at the corner of 52nd Street and Greenwood Avenue. To me as a child, it seemed to be among the biggest buildings in the world.

Of course, I had seen other large buildings that reduced ours to relative insignificance; especially the huge hulking skyscrapers of downtown Chicago that dwarfed everything else in the city. But in my neighborhood, our building was king. And in my mind, its size was further swelled by the pride I had in knowing that my father had owned it until his death, made it what it was, and had passed it on to us as part of his estate.

In all, Frank Turner Sr. had owned seven similar buildings and left quite a real estate fortune to his wife and family upon his death. By material standards, our life was comfortable and luxurious. We wore the finest clothes; we owned the finest cars and my sisters and I attended private schools.

> Frank Turner Sr. had left quite a fortune to his family upon his death.

As a child, I can't remember wanting for anything financial or material, though I do recall instances where my mother was apparently threatened by people to whom she owed gambling debts and wasn't paying them promptly enough.

Our apartment was a spacious English style flat with a wonderful view overlooking the corner. It was on what is generally called the first floor of many Chicago neighborhood buildings, even though technically the first floor was the above ground basement, that gave the building its first twelve feet of height.

To me the apartment was made for a kid because of its long hallway connecting the sun parlor and living room at the front end to the large dining room and well equipped kitchen at the other.

It was a hallway ideal for running; a long, super runway fit for the takeoff of imaginary jets; a soccer run for a future World

Cup superstar; and a suitable flight path for Superman (Superboy, really) to reach his tiny fortress of solitude behind the sofa after a long flight from the backdoor.

There were two large bedrooms at each end of the apartment. One, even with the living room, that had a door off the foyer. That was mine. The other room was slightly smaller with its own bathroom that sat just off the kitchen and was shared by my sisters.

A third bedroom sat off the middle of the long hallway across from the bathroom. That was my mother's. It was a master bedroom, with its own walk-in closet in which her furs and fine evening gowns were stored. My mother would often find me hiding, or napping in there, surrounded in the darkness by the velvety soft wonder of her precious things.

> When my mother died, I had just turned six years old.

When my mother died in March of 1966, I had just turned six years old in December. My sisters were fifteen and sixteen years old and found immediate avenues of escape. My older sister went off to stay with relatives in Oklahoma and my oldest sister, within months, was headed off to college in Iowa.

My mother had never wanted our grandmother to have custody of her children in the event of her death. She already knew what I was soon to learn about the dangers of being left in the care of her mother.

She thought she had prepared for any eventual dilemma

by pressuring a close friend into an agreement to take care of us if necessary. But the promise made by my mother's friend was empty and when the time came to step up and take responsibility for me, she took off instead.

That left me alone with my grandmother. She moved into our apartment from hers across the hall. And overnight, the one I had always known as a sweet, gentle, wonderful woman became a monster. Everything changed.

What has now popularly become known as child abuse, during my childhood was called discipline, and it was brutal in my home. Or rather, what instantly became my grandmother's home; a horrid place where she ruled with an iron will, a powerful hand and a closed mind; a place where she was a vicious and quite ambitious prosecutor, while I was always the ill fated defendant: without counsel, often unsure of my crime and certain every time to be convicted.

> What has now become known as child abuse, during my childhood was called discipline.

My grandmother had a temper that could frighten even the devil and it whipped up faster than a killer tornado. It was also just as deadly. Grandmother had no qualms about handing out the harshest sentences of the most vicious beatings for even the smallest offenses.

She was in her late fifties or early sixties when my mother died. No one can be sure because she always lied about her age. She was about 100 pounds overweight and though not very tall, she was still a very intimidating giant from my tiny perspective.

With my sisters gone, I was moved into the back bedroom and Grandmother moved into the front one. The middle bedroom that had been my mother's was closed and locked. There was a special deadbolt Grandmother had installed with its single key never out of her grasp.

I was told to never even think of entering that room again under penalty of being tried and convicted of trespassing. I was never again to feel the soft velvety wonder of my mother's furs or other precious belongings; never to smell the scent of her that still lingered in many of her things; never to know the peace and solitude of her dark cedar closet.

No, these wonderful comforts were to be replaced by a new and terrorizing image: that of my mother as a *ghost*.

Grandmother would tell me daily how my mother's room was haunted by her disembodied spirit; that she had seen visions of my mother hovering in the room and that it was being kept locked for my own protection, though she might consent to throwing me in there and letting my mother's haunting spirit "deal with me" if it was ever necessary.

Even as a frightened little boy, my conscious mind could never be convinced that my mother would ever hurt me in any way, let alone torment me from beyond the grave. But in my sleep there was no such reasoning. My subconscious created all sorts of "Mommy Monsters" that chased and threatened me from sleep, and filled my days with guilt for having the terrible nightmares about my mother, over which I had no control.

For years, my most restful sleep was always during the light of day.

Shortly after the locking of my mother's room and the final physical separation of me from all of her personal things, I found myself even more dependent on Grandmother for attention, love and affection.

In a bizarre way, Grandmother dished out affection as easily as she dished out terror. She could be beating me to within an inch of my life one moment and then before my tears could dry, demanding I come into her outstretched open arms for a warm embrace.

That would also give me a chance to tell her I loved her.

When Grandmother, who always insisted on being called "Grandmother" or "Grandmother Dear," demanded to be told that I loved her, the response had to be immediate and *convincing* no matter how traumatized I might have been at the moment.

The punishment for insincerity was severe. If she felt she was being slighted in any way, the stiff penalty of a stiff backhand across the face could be immediately imposed.

She could bring terror and affection together in a seamless fashion that blurred where the joy of a moment would end and a tornado would suddenly stir up.

And then just as suddenly as it had started, the tornado would pass and in the emotional rubble of what was left in its wake, my confused little mind would try to rebuild on a new foundation of her renewed affection and demonstration of love; until the next time. And the next time would always come.

Hell's Kitchen

One of those times was about a year after my mother died. I had spent one of many customary afternoons standing at our kitchen sink on a step stool washing and drying dishes, glassware, pots and frying pans, bowls and cups, baking dishes and virtually everything else that could fit into the sink.

My grandmother spent the entire day supervising, with her favorite leather strap. It was a long strip of tanned leather about the length of a belt, but considerably thicker and with no buckle. Other than beating me, I never knew what its intended purpose was.

Frank as a child.

As usual I washed and dried as fast as I could and the occasional but predictable sting of a smack across my bottom, shoulders or the back of my head from that strap kept the production line moving. I tried to set a pace that would stop Grandmother from hitting me; not as much to avoid the pain which was considerable, but more to stem the humiliation.

She would yell as she struck me and I would cry as I was hit. Both her yells and my crying could be heard clearly through the kitchen window she insisted remain open so that the children playing on the stairs of our building's back porch could hear me.

It would become impossible for them to resist the sideshow and they would always stop whatever game they were playing and I was missing, to become gawkers at the wreckage of my tortured life. The sting of their giggles and laughter at my expense hurt even more than the sting of that strap.

It was a scene and a circumstance more often repeated than I care to remember, but on this particular occasion was followed by a uniquely bizarre occurrence.

At about 3:00 the next morning I was awakened from a deep sleep by the sting of that strap across my back.

Even as the burning of my flesh began to arouse me from slumber, it took a moment to register that the pain from the blows that were now striking me head to toe as I instinctively flinched and writhed in my bed, was not part of a dream but rather a nightmare from the reality of my grandmother's completely disturbed mind.

She was standing over me, reigning blows down upon me,

slinging that leather strap and yelling at the top of her lungs for me to get out of bed and into the kitchen.

> The pain from the blows was a nightmare from the reality of my grandmother's completely disturbed mind.

With her literally herding me into the kitchen with that strap, I saw a sight which left me astonished and more confused than I had ever been in my young life.

The kitchen sink was full; full and overflowing onto the counter tops. Full with every pot and pan, every dish, plate, saucer and cup, every glass and container, every knife, fork and spoon; every single item I had spent that entire beautiful sunny spring afternoon getting beaten and humiliated standing on a stool at the sink washing, scrubbing and drying. Every sparkling clean item had been piled back into the sink.

And my grandmother kept insisting that I admit I had never washed any of them, peppering each request with another prompt from that strap. It was several more blows before I understood; several more blows before I gave up the futile attempt to reason with her, to remind her of how I had washed and dried them all while she had stood there right beside me "supervising."

As she repeatedly asked me to admit I had never washed the dishes, any of them, and as I continued to insist I had, taking a blow with each denial, it became clear that the only way to escape the situation with my life, or even escape being beaten to within an inch of it, was to confess the lie she wanted to hear.

There was no time to ponder the endless list of psychotic possibilities for her behavior that included sneaking into the kitchen in the middle of the night to pile the dishes back into the sink. There was no time to say anything but the words that might stop the blows. And so I said them.

I told her I lied, that I had never washed the dishes after all and that I was sorry. I felt like I was losing my little mind. I knew I was awake, but it felt like a bad dream.

The dishes I had washed, as if washing them while being publicly tortured in front of the peers I should have been out playing with wasn't enough, were all back in the sink, I was confessing that I had never washed them, and my false confession was appeasing my grandmother.

She stopped hitting me. She smiled at me. She told me I was a good boy for telling the truth. And then she told me to get busy washing those dishes.

And so I did. It took the rest of the night. I had to hurry so I could be finished in time to get ready for school. The last thing I wanted to do was make my grandmother mad by being late for school.

Making the Grade

There was another time that was just as confusing and just as typical; just as indicative of what life with my grandmother was like on a daily basis. Whether asleep or awake, you were always having a nightmare.

I have been blessed with a natural ability to read, and by the time I started kindergarten I could read, if not fully comprehend just about any material at a middle school, even high school level.

On the day that third grade final report cards were being handed out, I was told that a meeting would be necessary between my grandmother and the school principal. Unlike most meetings between principals and parents, the occasion was to be a happy one. Grandmother would be informed, as I was, that in the fall I would be promoted to fifth grade instead of fourth. My report card showed final grades of four A's and one B.

I was supposedly given the B in English because of the one word I had missed on my final spelling test by carelessly transposing a couple of letters in my haste to finish quickly. It was the only time I had gotten less than a 100% score on a spelling quiz.

Arriving home on the last formal day of school with my report card proudly in hand, I was positive this was a day with no risk. Grandmother, I was sure, would be as thrilled as I. She might even hug me and give me one of those warm smiles, and perhaps even tell me she was proud of me.

She was indeed thrilled that I was going to be skipped a grade, until she got a look at the actual report card. All she could see was that B staring at her and she was incensed.

A classmate whom I was occasionally allowed to play with was also being skipped a grade. Before I had gotten home, his mother had called my grandmother to share congratulations over the good news. During their conversation the woman had also gloated over the fact that her son had gotten *all* A's but added that my grandmother should nonetheless be just as proud of my accomplishment.

Grandmother wasn't exactly clear on just what that meant until I arrived home with the report card that, as she put it, *confirmed her humiliation.*

She saw the B and I got one of the worst beatings I ever experienced. The funny thing is that I don't remember the pain from the strap as much as the words from her mouth.

She told me I was worthless and disgraceful, that I was embarrassing and stupid, and that I would never amount to anything. She told me that because of me, she would never be able to show her face around that school

> She told me I was worthless and disgraceful, and that I would never amount to anything.

and that my classmate's family was laughing at her. She said she was humiliated and it was entirely my fault.

As it turned out, I *had rightfully* earned all A's. The teacher later admitted to my grandmother that the principal had switched my English grade with the grade of the other boy being promoted, who was white, so that he would not appear inferior.

As far as my grandmother was concerned, it was as if the revelation had never been made. She never ceased using that incident to remind me of her *humiliation* and my *failure* and she never acknowledged that she had been wrong.

Boy in the 'Hood

I indeed had a miserable life but I lived in a wonderful neighborhood.

Hyde Parkers were an eclectic mixture of University professors and faculty, judges and lawyers, doctors and nurses, postal workers, school teachers, bus drivers, secretaries and clerks, mechanics and laborers.

In Hyde Park, you could find the very wealthy and the middle class. A man who owned a factory might live just a few blocks away from men who worked on his production line; a store owner not far from his clerks and cashiers, private school students waited at the bus stops with public school teachers.

In the spring and summer, lawns were green, manicured, and well watered. Large oak trees lined and shaded big portions of the streets. The concrete sidewalks were even and kept clean, though often decorated with the colorful chalk outline of someone's last game of hopscotch.

On the rare occasions when my grandmother would actually allow me to go outside to play, sometimes I would just sit on the curb and stare.

I would get caught up in listening to the rustling of the leaves while the warm gentle wind of a Chicago summer, far too short not to be savored, caressed my skin as it carried the fresh aroma of fruit and flowers from a backyard nearby.

The neighbors in the townhouses usually had fruit trees growing in their yards, and several times my friends and I were chased out of them after stuffing ourselves with stolen pears, apples, cherries and mulberries.

Hyde Park Boulevard was a busy and sometimes noisy thoroughfare. Giant green city buses, "Big Green Limousines" we used to call them, rumbled loudly along the street while spewing the rancid exhaust from their diesel fuel; their stops always announced by the screeching and squealing of their brakes.

But Greenwood, the side street on which I lived, ran off of the boulevard and my corner was very peaceful. As a young child, I remember it being the epitome of the neighborhood itself, quiet and relatively crime free. People walked comfortably and without fear on summer nights and children played freely, their parents unencumbered by worries of abductions or molestations by strangers.

> Everyone knew everybody else *and* everybody else's business.

You knew the owner of almost every car you saw and sometimes just hearing the noise it made was the only clue you needed. Everyone knew everybody else *and* everybody else's business.

But by the time I was about ten, the neighborhood was already changing. More of the upper middle class and wealthy moved out and more working poor families headed by single mothers moved in. Gang activity grew, drug dealing increased, and people who still walked at night were more careful to look over their shoulders at the sound of approaching footsteps.

And it was exactly some of the people they would've been most frightened to see walking behind them who suddenly seemed *cool* to me.

I got my first real "high" from beer and marijuana hanging out with these older boys in my neighborhood. I was fourteen, and in the spring of 1974 was also feeling another kind of intoxication. It was the intoxication of freedom.

My oldest sister had gone to court to win custody of me from my grandmother and rescue me from the years of emotional, verbal, physical and unknown to her, sexual abuse.

I was moving from Chicago to live with her in Cedar Rapids, Iowa as soon as school was out in June; and so that spring was a season of emancipation. Grandmother's hold over me had been broken. I was no longer afraid of her and my escape had been secured.

Armed with my new freedom and the courage of knowing my escape was certain, I went wild. I went completely wild. I went completely, totally, off-the-deep end, uncontrollably hog wild.

> I went completely, totally, off-the-deep end, uncontrollably hog wild.

I went out when I felt like it, to go wherever I chose; I stayed out as long as I wanted, and did anything and everything without restraint.

I was only fourteen, but I acted like forty and carried the burden, pain and heartbreak of a man who'd seen twice that many years. I had a giant hole in my heart and an even bigger chip on my shoulder and I lived life as a dare to someone, anyone, to try and knock it off.

These older boys, the *real cool* guys in the neighborhood, boys in their late teens who thought like children and looked like men; boys that a year earlier I wouldn't have gone near suddenly became magnets that irresistibly drew me to them.

Growing up with two older sisters and a grandmother and without a father, I had not been accustomed to the attention and influence of older male figures, except for those my grandmother had allowed to rape and molest me; hanging out with these guys made me feel powerful, accepted and *normal*. I was certain, at least then, that these were people who'd never been abused, beaten or sodomized as I had been.

They cursed and drank and smoked and got into fights. They were muscular and cocky and rude. They were tough and they were cool.

They were also products of broken and poverty ravaged homes and neglected public education, so as a child of relative wealth and private school privilege I was miles ahead socially and intellectually, but they were still my heroes.

Ironically, it would be much later in life before I understood that child abuse, neglect and molestation are universal; and that the behavior of these boys had probably been shaped by the very same kind of childhood traumas I had suffered.

It was with these boys, these icons of influence, that I

first discovered the "high" life.

Laughter is the Best Medicine

"Hey, you wanna hit this?"

I remember one of "the boys" asking me that as if it was yesterday. I can still hear his voice in my head. Of course that was the night I heard a lot of voices in my head.

I'll never forget the balmy summer-like breeze of that warmer than usual spring night, the fluorescent glow of the streetlight casting an eerie greenish illumination onto the darkened swing set area of the concrete playground, and my utter shock at one of "the boys" asking, "Hey, you wanna hit this?"

I didn't answer. I couldn't answer. My tongue was a frozen solid hunk of meat and my lips were sewn shut.

At least that's how it felt.

But it didn't matter that my mouth suddenly didn't work. After all, I thought, it wasn't even possible that he was talking to me anyway. The only thing anybody should've been saying to me was "Beat it!"

"Yo slim, I'm talkin' to you man. Do you wanna hit this or not?"

What?! Could he really be talking to me? Oh my God!

In that moment, time seemed to stretch a single second into an eternity, while a thousand thoughts raced through my head at lightning speed. *Do I want to hit it? Of course I want to hit it! I don't know how to hit it! What's going to happen when I hit it? If*

I don't say something, this guy's gonna think I'm retarded. What exactly does it mean to "hit" it?

The "it" was a joint (that's a hand-rolled marijuana cigarette for the uninitiated) that had just been lit and "the boys" were passing "it" around.

I had smelled the sweet yet particularly pungent aroma of burning marijuana on a few occasions, but had never actually seen the stuff. I'd seen "the boys" smoking it before rolled up in ultra-thin, yellow colored rice paper that turned an exotic green as it burned, but never dreamed of the possibility of this moment when I was in the midst of "the boys" *while* they were smoking it and one of them was *passing* it to me.

As I reached out for the joint, pretending to have a casual ease as if it was something I did several times a day (which, actually did soon happen) I felt everything going in slow motion. Voices seemed to slow to a dragging drawl and everyone seemed to be moving as if we were in a video stuck on pause and having the frames of motion advanced one at a time, but my *mind* was now racing even faster than before.

It occurred to me in that moment that not only had I never smoked marijuana, I had never smoked *anything*! I didn't *really* know how to take a "hit!"

When I was about seven or eight years old I'd taken a cigarette from the pack of Winston's sticking out of the purse of a lady who often came by to "clean" my grandmother's apartment. My grandmother kept her apartment so junky and cluttered that actual cleaning wasn't really possible, so all the lady could do was move stuff from one place to another and try to vacuum and dust around it.

Anyway, I took a cigarette from her pack, grabbed a book of matches from the kitchen drawer and slipped out onto the back porch while Grandmother was busy harassing the lady for not "cleaning" hard enough.

I'd seen plenty of smoking in fantasy and reality. Everybody featured on screens large and small, whether hero or villain, smoked. Everybody I thought was cool in real life smoked. Everybody I saw with a cigarette always looked so satisfied, so content, like they were sucking down the pure enjoyment of life instead of just toxic carcinogens.

I put the filter tip to my lips and clamped down on it like I'd seen in movies and television shows and then struck the match. I held the fire to the end of the cigarette and sucked in.

But that's where imitation left off and self preservation kicked in.

If the body knows one thing for sure it's that it doesn't like smoke. I didn't know how to inhale the smoke and I didn't want to swallow it, but I ended up kind of doing both while my body was doing everything it could to keep me from doing either.

I was choking, hacking and spitting from the smoke going down my throat, and my eyes were watering and burning from the smoke going up my nose and down into my lungs. Everything felt like it was on fire.

My body was shaking so uncontrollably from the coughing I must have looked like I was having a seizure and in the process I knocked the fire off the cigarette and burned myself.

And with that being my only smoking experience—my only previous attempt to take a "hit" off something—here I was in the last place in the world I wanted to look like a fool, taking a joint I didn't know what to do with, from the hand of one of "the boys" I wanted to impress the most.

Let's Hit It!

I was determined in this moment that I would not be the fool. No matter what the cost to be paid or the pain to be endured, I had a shot at being "cool" for the first time and I was not going to blow it.

I'd watched when the joint was lit. I tried not to stare, but I had watched carefully as the fire was sucked in to the tip of it from the match and the smoke drawn straight and deep into the lungs.

I'd watched as it was passed a couple of times, each person carefully squeezing the tip of the joint between their thumb and forefinger to shield it from being soaked in saliva as they pressed their puckered lips tightly against it.

I'd watched the pained expression on their faces as each tried to hold in the acrid, hot and harsh smoke deep in their lungs and the shuddering sigh as it was exhaled in a long slow rushing bluish cloud of relief.

And I'd watched them smoke before and heard the occasional gagging cough as someone invariably tried to hold in too much smoke for too long and had to fight the body's natural impulse to expel the smoke out of the lungs.

I'd seen enough to imitate and I was determined enough to look like I knew what I was doing. But at this point the thought that smoking the joint might actually *have an effect* on *me* was the farthest thing from my mind.

My only concern was to look cool; to look like I belonged and fit in; to look like one of "the boys" and I was determined that no matter what that smoke tasted like or how much it burned my throat and lungs or how violently my body tried to reject it, *I was going to hit that joint.*

And so I did. I squeezed the tip of the joint between my thumb and forefinger and pressed it tightly against my puckered lips and sucked as hard as I could; drawing a steady stream of hot, bitter, harsh smoke directly and deeply into my lungs.

As the muscles in my throat closed off my smoke-filled lungs and my teeth clenched and lips tightened, I casually passed off the smoldering stick of weed to the next man.

I was holding in the smoke. I wasn't choking; I wasn't gagging. I wasn't blowing my shot at being one of "the boys." I was holding in the smoke.

I was cool.

With every fiber of my being I was holding steady, determined not to shudder or quake. If it meant my death, I would not choke or sputter, gag or spit. But I had held the smoke for so long that, deprived of oxygen, I was in danger of passing out and so it was time for the moment of truth; the moment of victory and the ultimate moment of "cool."

As I let go with a shuddering sigh and the smoke was exhaled in a long slow rushing bluish cloud of relief, my brain swelled, and my mind took off like a rocket while my head tightened. My vision blurred and the sound in my head began to roar and echo, and suddenly everything felt warm and tingly.

I knew the word *euphoria,* but I'd never felt it until now and I was completely overwhelmed by it. I was *high* as a kite and felt completely out of control and like I suddenly didn't have a care in the world.

> In that sudden rush of marijuana induced ecstasy I was unburdened and unleashed.

In that sudden rush of marijuana-induced ecstasy, I was unburdened and unleashed and everything in the world at that moment seemed...funny.

Yes, funny.

And so, I laughed. I laughed hard; *really, really* hard.

It wasn't a titter, or a giggle, or merely a chuckle. It wasn't really even something that you could confine within the boundaries of a "guffaw."

No, what sprayed out of me in that instant was rapturous, rumbling, *eruption-from-deep-in-my-belly-and-exploding-from-my-lips-like-a-volcano* laughter.

It was wild, it was ecstatic, it was unusual laughter. It was strange, it was frightening, it was bewildering laughter. It was *maybe-we-better-get-some-help-for-this-kid, this-is-gonna-end-*

my-cool-career laughter.

I laughed like an out-of-control fool. I never in my life felt more stupid, but I honestly never to that point had felt better. I felt so happy, so filled with a sense of joy, so overwhelmed by peace and satisfaction, so…amused.

I just kept laughing. But in my mind I was also thinking: I can't stop. This laughing feels good, but it's also out of control. I realized that I wasn't trying to laugh or even at first wanting to laugh, but that being "high" on the marijuana was *making* me laugh and I actually couldn't stop. And *then* I realized…I didn't want to.

You see, I hadn't laughed in years. Not like this. Not with this much freedom, not with this much abandon, not with this much *euphoria*. I was laughing from a part of me that I didn't know was still inside me.

I was laughing from a part of me I thought had been sealed in the casket with my mother before they put her in the ground.

> I was laughing from a part of me I thought had been beaten out of me.

I was laughing from a part of me I thought had been beaten out of me by the unrelenting lashes from my grandmother's leather straps, shoes, belts, ironing and extension cords and broom handles.

I was laughing from a part of me I thought had been drained out of me by the endless acts of rape and molestation I had endured from the age of eight.

I was laughing from a part of me I thought had been cut out of me by the razor-sharp words that had been wielded as weapons by my grandmother to confirm her contempt for my birth and her anger that I was taking up space and breathing air in what without me, in her view, would be a perfect world.

I was laughing from a place that only this drug could reach inside of me and find and pull to the surface. And so I laughed. And I didn't care what anybody thought.

But here's the funny part: "the boys" I was so worried about impressing; "the boys" I was so concerned about being embarrassed in front of; the *super-cool, king-of-the-neighborhood, hard-as-nails boys* I was so determined not to disappoint were laughing so hard they were crying.

They weren't laughing *with* me and had no idea what I was laughing about, but they were laughing *at* me so hard they didn't care. This astounding and yet strange immediate effect that marijuana had on me was the best entertainment any of them had ever seen.

Marijuana makes just about everyone kind of silly initially, though its effect on me was rather dramatic. But under its influence and with me cackling uncontrollably, the hardest guys in the neighborhood were weak as kittens and doubled over in hysterical laughing fits.

A while later, when we (mostly me) were all able to calm down, "the boys" told me they had never seen anybody "trippin' like that!" They asked me if that happened every time I got high. I told them this was the first time. But I knew it was going to be the first of many.

We anted up on some beer, which under the spell of the marijuana and the dry parched "cotton-mouth" it causes, was remarkably thirst-quenching but more notably it was quite intoxicating.

It made me think of my uncle and his prediction. I knew he had been wrong; that I would never develop a "taste" for beer. But by the end of that night, I knew I would develop a tolerance for it because I immediately fell head over heels for the effect of it.

I tolerated the taste of beer for only one reason: intoxication. As a young teenager, I found out that beer could get you "high" and that I liked the "high" life.

That warm spring night in 1974, when I was fourteen years old, my head found an answer my heart had been searching for since I was six. I got high on pot and drunk on beer and laughed like a fool.

My heart was still aching, but my head didn't feel it. I was giddy, I was numb, I had discovered a general anesthetic and for the first time since my mother's death, I was feeling no pain.

> I had discovered the answer to a broken heart was an intoxicated mind.

I had discovered the answer to a broken heart was an intoxicated mind. That night, I dedicated myself to the full exploration of discovering just how high a person could get.

I determined that I had nothing to lose. I couldn't go back to the heartache, not after the joy and the chemically induced euphoria, which I had no idea was counterfeit.

No, I had to go forward. I had to become a pioneer of sorts. Like others who had sailed uncharted oceans, blazed trails across unsettled territories and blasted off into the undiscovered reaches of space; I was determined to discover and explore the farthest reaches of the "high."

> If my indulgence of any drug would cost my life, then so be it.

I pledged to get as high as possible and go as deep as necessary. I was willing to take any risk and pay any price. And if my indulgence of any drug would cost my life, then so be it.

I pledged that when that moment came, I would use my dying breath to thank whatever was killing me for the sweet release.

Better Living Through Chemistry

Just a year later, I had developed several addictions and a personal motto: if you can smoke it, toke it, snort it, pop it or pour it, you can pass it…to me.

Just a year after *discovering* the "high" life, I was *immersed* in it, engulfed by it and hooked on it.

Just a year into the "high" life, I installed myself as the life-long president of the *get-as-high-as-you-can* club which actually served to shorten the lives of its members.

Just a year later, I was willing to take *anything* from *anybody*. It wasn't long before I was completely indiscriminate about my chemical consumption. I was ingesting amphetamines and methamphetamines, barbiturates and opiates, hallucinogens like mescaline and LSD, and I was "huffing" (inhaling) toxins like chemical cleaners and solvents.

On a daily basis, I was dropping acid and popping speed, taking Quaaludes, smoking pot and hash, and drinking beer. I was always cruising, tripping, flying and crashing. I was taking anything that promised a "high" and it didn't matter where it came from, whether prescription or homemade.

In high school, there were kids who'd stay up all night making powders and pills in their basements with their amateur scientist chemistry sets. They'd offer me a trial of their latest experiment suggesting that I take "half" of one thing or another.

I'd say, "Give me two of 'em! Let's see if they *really* work!" And I'd drop a double dose.

I was so reckless, it didn't occur to me that I was popping the homemade pills of kids who I knew for certain *were flunking chemistry!*

Just a year later, that was my life. It was the "high" life that began in 1974, when I was fourteen years old, on one unforgettable night in the playground down the street from our apartment, when the boys I thought were the coolest things walking, finally turned their attention my way.

When the World Cracked

It was February of 1977 and I had just turned seventeen in December. I was standing in the kitchen of a childhood friend, with whom I had recently reconnected, and at that moment I was contemplating the murder of her boyfriend.

> At that moment I was contemplating the murder of her boyfriend.

Seconds earlier, he had taken the rather substantial amount of cocaine I had just pulled out of my pocket, poured a lot of it into a glass test tube and then poured an ounce of water in on top of it.

I remember looking at a set of kitchen knives sitting on the counter near me and mentally choosing which one would be in my hand when I dove over the counter to plunge it into his chest.

I had no idea what he was doing or why he was apparently just ruining my very expensive packet of cocaine, but he must have been able to sense that I was thinking it was a capital offense, because he looked at me, put his hand up in a halting motion and said, "Take it easy. Everything will be alright. When I'm done, you'll love me."

Needless to say, I was already fairly obsessive about cocaine. I had been snorting it for a couple of years in ever increasing amounts and occasionally went on binges, even snorting it until my nose bled.

On this particular night, I had purchased what was at that point the largest single amount I'd ever planned to put right up my nose: an eighth of an ounce, which at that time was nearly $400 worth.

I had taken it out to snort a few lines and perhaps share a little with my friend, when her boyfriend asked if he could check out the packet. That's why I handed it to him.

For the moment, I put his execution on hold and stood there in amazement and watched what he did. With the test tube held in one hand by the rim, he carefully took a measured amount of baking soda and sifted it into the tube.

> For the moment, I put his execution on hold.

Then he took the cocaine, water and baking soda mixture and started "cooking" it by swirling the bottom of the test tube around over the open flame of the gas stovetop.

It was like watching some kind of mad scientist! I had never seen anything like it before and I had been around a lot of drugs and seen people do some very weird things with them. But this was the most fascinating drug demonstration I had ever witnessed.

As he swirled the test tube over the flame, the powder mixture of cocaine and baking soda dissolved completely in the water, bubbled up briefly into a frothy fizz, and then seemed to disappear.

And then things got really weird.

He opened the fridge, took out a glass of water with several ice cubes floating in it and set it on the counter and then grabbed a teaspoon. First he poured two teaspoons of the ice water into the test tube then he put the bottom of the tube into the water to cool it off further.

When he pulled it out again I could see a gooey substance floating around at the bottom of the tube. It was the cocaine! By "cooking" it, he had purified and concentrated it. The processing that had turned the drug from a kind of "sap" originally found in the coca plant, into the powder I had purchased, had been reversed.

He poured a few more drops of ice water into the tube and then picked up a section of a wire coat hanger that he had broken off, and stuck it down to the bottom of the tube and gently stirred.

I was spellbound!

As he gently swirled the tip of the wire coat hanger section down into the "goo" it began to cling to the tip of the hanger! Then this "goo" started to turn from a transparent glob into a milky white hardened "rock" that was stuck to the tip of the hanger.

By this time I had completely forgotten that I had even come over to get high! I was just stunned and staring. It was like watching one of those "Mr. Science" shows on TV, only a lot more strange and compelling.

He put the "rock" onto a plate, took a razor blade and shaved off a small chunk and placed it into the bowl of a glass pipe that I hadn't even noticed sitting on the kitchen table.

For years, I had used just about every kind of pipe

imaginable for smoking marijuana, but this was obviously different. It had a long and slender neck and the "rock" was sitting in the bowl of it which was filled with copper wire "screens."

He handed me the pipe. My initial rage had long since given way to fascination and now utter confusion. I prided myself on being "cool" in those days and it just wasn't cool to have no idea what you were doing when it came to drugs. But it was obvious that I didn't have a clue.

But what happened next changed my life forever. He took another piece of broken off wire coat hanger about six inches long and carefully wrapped a white cotton ball around the tip of it. Then he half filled a glass with grain alcohol. At first I thought he was offering me a drink and believe me, I would have taken it.

> What I saw and did next changed my life forever.

But the grain alcohol was 180 proof and very flammable. He dipped the cotton ball on the end of the length of coat hanger into the grain alcohol and soaked it, then pressed it against the inside of the glass to squeeze off the excess. When he held it to the flame on the stove it ignited with a muffled "whoosh" and became a miniature torch.

He told me to put the pipe to my lips and then draw deeply from it, slowly and steadily, as he held the torch so that the flame gently kissed the "rock" in the bowl of the pipe.

The "rock" of cocaine began to crackle and sputter as it melted under the intense heat. While I inhaled deeply, the melting "rock" turned to smoke that filled the chamber of the clear glass pipe on its way into my lungs. When my lungs were filled to capacity, I pulled the pipe from my lips and he blew out the torch.

Holding my breath and clenching my teeth, I mumbled a robotic sounding, "Now what?"

He said, "Hold it in as long as you can, and then blow it out."

I'll never forget those words. "Hold it in as long as you can, and then blow it out."

It was a milestone. It was a turning point. It was a remarkable watershed moment that caused another division by which my life was forever divided into "before" and "after."

They were the last words spoken to me before I fell off a cliff into a seemingly bottomless pit of addiction. They were the last words spoken to the Frank Turner who died that day and would never be seen again. They were the last words that were spoken to me before I became a stone-cold, cocaine-junkie, crack-head.

> I fell off a cliff into a seemingly bottomless pit of addiction.

"Hold it in as long as you can, and then blow it out."

Not being one who was willing to ignore any instruction that would maximize a "high" from a drug, especially one I was using for the first time, I followed the instruction quite literally.

I held the smoke of purified, concentrated, unadulterated cocaine in my lungs until I actually could not hold it one second longer, and then I blew it out.

As the smoke rushed from my lungs with a forceful exhale, the person I had been to that point rushed out with it.

In an instant, as the smoke poured out of my body, I changed into a person buried deep inside me that I never knew existed; someone I would come to intimately know yet never really understand; someone for whom death would become the meaning and purpose of life.

"Hold it in as long as you can, and then blow it out."

I heard those words as one person, and by obeying them, became another.

Now, with my lungs emptying of the smoke and my mind filling with its effects, it was as if both I and the world I came from ceased to exist, and I was a stranger, even to myself, floating out into space.

Or so it seemed. But I was not floating, I was falling and it was not into space but off a cliff. With the first hit from that pipe, I had stepped off a cliff and was falling into a deep, dark pit. It would take twenty-two years to hit the bottom.

Hooked on a Feeling

Describing the basic effect of smoking pure cocaine seems almost flippant in its simplicity: it just changes you.

It changes the traits hidden deep within your inner recesses into your outward behavior, your inner secrets become your outward expressions, and the person you never admitted you were becomes the personality whose emergence cannot be denied.

In essence it changes you——by turning you inside out.

Cocaine kills the personality you've been by unleashing the personality you've repressed and it forces you to expose the vulnerable parts of your inner self that your mind had taken great pains to conceal.

From the first hit off the pipe you are left exposed by the controls that no longer remain, the inhibitions rendered inoperative and the limits that no longer exist. You become desperate to do what otherwise you would not and unable to resist what otherwise would not even be of interest.

> Cocaine kills the personality you've been by unleashing the personality you've repressed.

The effect of smoking cocaine is the trap for which the feeling of smoking it is the bait. The feeling is more complex and difficult to describe.

The difficulty in describing the feeling from smoking pure cocaine is that it can be likened to so many sensory experiences but no other single experience is adequate to capture the fullness of the intoxication.

It begins with something akin to an extreme euphoria, but the intensity level soon rockets right past euphoria with a blazing acceleration into a region where "euphoric" is no longer a fitting adjective. In that place, there is an explosion of intense but synthetic satisfaction—a free-flowing giddiness that floods the brain and body with an overwhelming sensation of false serenity.

The feeling also includes an intense and tingling

numbness—a full body, head-to-toe anesthetization that digs down into the soul to deaden the deepest of repressed wounds and heartaches even as it simultaneously dredges up these injuries for further emotional exploration.

And then there is the powerful manipulation of the libido which leads to the irresistible desire to explore the hidden longings of the flesh, even those which are harvested by the mind as the forbidden fruit of seeds that were painfully sown through abuse and molestation.

It is a combination of feelings—a tantalizing sensory cocktail of death that draws you in, holds you down and then starts to squeeze the very breath of life from your soul even as it begins to set itself up as the replacement for all that it is extinguishing.

> The initial satisfaction becomes the inevitable suffocation.

The numbness which tempted you becomes its own brand of pain to torture you. Suddenly, your insatiable hunger is for nothing but the cocaine itself. The libidinous desires it once ignited are eventually dowsed in the inability to crave anything but the drug. And that which seemed like serenity is revealed as the perpetual torment of an addiction that cannot be broken.

Drawn into its depths, you begin to drown and the initial satisfaction becomes the inevitable suffocation.

CHAPTER THREE

***

A MOMENT OF TRUTH

"And you shall know the truth, and the truth shall make you free" (John 8:32).

More than twenty-one years from that moment of truth, when my mother was forced to confess to her husband, Frank Turner Sr., that she was pregnant with me, there was another moment of truth that made all of my life to that point make sense.

It was a moment of clarity, a moment of revelation, a bright and shining and yet dark and disturbing moment of truth that knocked the wind right out of me.

It was an afternoon in 1980, on my twenty-first birthday and I was sitting at the kitchen table in the apartment where I grew up. It had been my grandmother's home since my mother's death and she was sitting there with me.

There was also a giant elephant in the room. Actually it was a photograph she had placed on the table in front of me, but it seemed like an elephant and it felt like he was standing on my chest.

I picked up the photo and stared at it. It was almost like a mirror held up to my face. It was my face looking back at me and yet it wasn't me at all. The man in the picture was older but his face was mine. His clothes were a different vintage but his face was mine. The picture was black and white, obviously weathered and aged and could not possibly be of me and yet, the face staring back at me from the photo was mine.

The elephant standing on my chest forced the wind out of me and sucked all the rest of the air out of the room. I sat there in a vacuum, unable to breathe, but for the first time, able to see. This moment of truth revealed so many things and—while it seemed to be choking off my air—it was opening my eyes.

After I forced enough air into my lungs to exhale a question, I asked the silliest question with the most obvious answer. The picture said it all, but I wanted to hear it from the lips of my grandmother. I needed to hear it spoken as a truth; I needed to have it confirmed as a fact, and I needed to have it exposed as the dirty little secret that had been hanging over my life like a dark cloud.

"Who is this?" I asked.

My grandmother said, "It's your father."

As I looked back down at the photo once again resting on the table in front of me, tears already filling the wells of my eyes. I mumbled, "This isn't Frank Turner."

"Frank Turner isn't your father," she said matter-of-factly. "This is Oscar Green—your real father."

More than twenty-one years earlier, Frank Turner looked into the eyes of a woman and was told that a man named Oscar

Green had turned his world upside down and made all he thought was truth into a lie. Twenty-one years later, another woman was telling another Frank Turner the same thing.

The Truth About The Truth

"And you shall know the truth, and the truth shall make you free" (John 8:32).

At twenty-one years old, my world had turned completely upside down and inside out. Most of what I thought to be true was a lie. My mother's character was nothing like I had imagined. My father's identity was not what I had previously been told. And the circumstances of my birth were not what I had always believed.

In essence, my mother was not who I thought. My father was not who I thought. *I* was not who I thought.

As I left my grandmother's apartment, I felt like a match that had just been struck. My head was hot and burning and what seemed like a blazing fiery tingle was coursing through my body from head to toe.

> It was a moment of intense pain, heartache and confusion.

It was a moment of intense pain, heartache and confusion, and yet it was also a moment of illumination and enlightenment. It was a moment of crystal clarity. It was a moment of liberation.

Left: Frank as a young man.

Below: Frank's biological father, Oscar Green.

Above: Frank's mother, young Opratee Turner.

Frank's grandmother, Lynne Johnson

The truth is like a sharp blade with a precise cutting edge that can surgically repair, critically wound or utterly destroy. It all depends upon who is wielding it and with what motive.

But knowing the truth will always set you free. And in that moment I was set free. I was free to remember and consider Opratee Turner as the real, living and imperfect human being that she was, instead of the saint my fond memories had made her.

I was free to reflect upon Frank Turner Sr. as the wounded, betrayed husband of an adulteress wife who apparently went to his grave heartbroken and yet wholeheartedly in love with his wife and the child of another man.

I was free to understand my sisters as the cheated half-sisters of an illegitimate child. I was free to understand the burning life-long resentment they shared, and at times couldn't hide, for me and for their mother, whose indiscretion produced me. And I was free to understand their resentment of my father, Oscar Green, the one of whom I am the spitting image.

And finally, I was free to begin to understand the years of abuse and neglect I suffered in the custody of my grandmother, my mother's mother who I discovered was actually in love with Frank Turner Sr., resentful of her daughter for taking him away from her, and hate-filled toward the grandson whose face reminded her daily of Frank Sr. being betrayed.

My grandmother had wielded the truth like a weapon, a knife to stab me in the back and a scalpel to cut through my heart. But that same weapon with which I was critically wounded was also a tool of liberation. It would be many years later before I would actually be able to walk in freedom but in that moment, long before I would realize it, it cut me free.

The truth had set me free. One day I would walk in that freedom. But it would not be this day.

Looking For Love in All the Wrong Places

I've hurt so many people because of the brokenness in my life and the pain in my heart. The love-hate relationship with the women who shaped my childhood became the basis for virtually all of my relationships with other women.

For much of my life I was obsessed with replacing the love of my mother. I craved being nurtured and longed for being needed. But her abandonment and death made me as afraid of actually depending on a woman's love as I was desperate to find it.

There was just as strong an effect from my traumatic relationship with my grandmother. She loved me in her heart and hated me in her mind. She loved me because I was her daughter's son, yet despised me for being Oscar Green's bastard child.

Her involvement in my sexual abuse and her disturbed patterns of beating me one minute, and then in the next minute demanding I hug and kiss her and tell her I loved her, ramped up my rage which I was then forced to repress.

Without even knowing why, I formed a clear pathological pattern in my pursuit and seduction of women. To me, every woman represented my mother whose affections had to be won at any cost; my grandmother who had to suffer my wrath of vengeance for her abuse; and a combination of the two, who had to be discarded before I could be hurt again.

I watched and was shaped by almost every woman I met. I studied them and I learned them. I listened to their longings and desires; I remembered their heartbreaks and recorded their responses to every situation.

I learned their frailties and their fears, what they wanted a man to say and do, how they longed for him to behave and what they dreamed he would desire and demand of them.

I learned their unfulfilled dreams and unmet expectations. I made mental notes of their needs to be respected, regarded and rewarded.

I learned so I could use what I knew to make women love me as a man on behalf of the six- year-old boy inside me who was trying to *replace* his mother and *punish* his grandmother.

In essence, I learned from these women how to be the perfect man. I learned how to be the most responsive and romantic, the most caring and compassionate, the most dedicated and devoted. I learned how to say what a woman wants to hear, do what a woman wants done and be what a woman wants to have.

> I could use what I knew to make women love me.

When a woman sought security, I promised it. When a woman expected exclusivity, I offered it. When a woman desired dedication, I provided the illusion of it.

And that became my pattern: seduce, punish, discard and abandon.

I would do anything to win a connection to a woman's heart, and when I had her, I'd do anything to cut it loose; the fear of losing her would force me to push her away before she had the chance to abandon me like my mother.

> That became my pattern: seduce, punish, discard, and abandon.

And in pushing her away, I had to hurt her as if to punish her for the hurt my grandmother caused me.

I went back and forth between seeking my mother, winning her love and then punishing my grandmother. It was impossible of course, to actually, authentically and truly love anyone by doing this. And so there were many romances but no relationships; plenty of promises, but no permanence.

And eventually, I wound up alone.

CHAPTER FOUR

THE BEGINNING OF THE END

For God will bring every work into judgment,
Including every secret thing,
Whether good or evil
(Ecclesiastes 12:14).

When I arrived in Detroit on October 9, 1990, I actually had a date with death but no idea it was looming on the horizon.

I didn't really know what to expect, but I had no basis to believe it was going to be good. Success wasn't really an option because I wasn't ready or able to abandon the addiction that had always brought failure.

Still, I was optimistic. Amazing what you can do with denial.

I had somehow talked myself into sincerely believing that it was going to be a new beginning. Looking back, I can see how it really was. It was the beginning of the end.

So much was happening all at once and my head was spinning.

I needed to find a home for my new family: my second wife, whom I had just married days earlier, and her adolescent son whose custody she had just been awarded after a battle with the boy's father.

I was equipped for neither marriage nor fatherhood, and exactly how I ended up taking on the responsibilities of both in the days before leaving New Orleans to come to Detroit remains a bit of a blur.

The Accidental Journalist

In many respects, the entire path that led to this point was a bit of a blur. I had done remarkably well in television journalism, particularly considering I never had any original ambitions of pursuing the field at all.

> I'd never been to journalism school and had never taken a news writing class.

In the early days of my career, I boastfully admitted that I'd never been to journalism school, had never taken a news writing class, and had originally attended college with the ambition of being an actor.

Just as boastfully, I had made it known that a career in television news had actually been a side benefit of my ability to sell water beds—yes, water beds.

I met the young man who turned out to be the catalyst for my accidental career while trying to sell him a water bed in a small store on Chicago's Near North Side. I had taken quite a winding road to meet him there.

After I was skipped from third to fifth grade, my

grandmother enrolled me in the prestigious University of Chicago Laboratory School. The move was more to gain status for her than to secure an educational opportunity for me. But the advantages of the accelerated curriculum later allowed me to graduate from high school in just three years.

I spent a year afterwards working as a waiter, a hotel doorman and dabbling in small-time drug dealing before deciding to go to college in preparation for becoming a writer, who could create roles for himself as an actor.

I was taking television production classes in college as background to prepare for acting, but they also put me in the same department as the young classmate who one day walked into the water bed store where I was working part-time.

As I sold him a bed, we became instant friends. And after a while he helped me get a "gopher" job (you know "go for" this and "go for" that) at WBBM-TV, the CBS station in Chicago, where he worked as a production assistant. That was the fancy TV newsroom name for gopher.

Instantly, I fell in love with the TV news business and learned everything I could about it by watching the reporters, anchors and writers do their work. Before long I had assembled my own audition tape of reporting and anchoring with their help.

Within a year, that first tape got me a job as a reporter for a TV station in Omaha, Nebraska, and the rest followed fairly easily. I never finished college. And only years later did I even remember my original ambition to go into acting.

It was clear from the beginning that I was, to use an old

cliché, a *natural*. I loved being in front of the camera and I loved

> **Being *infamous* was difficult but *famous* has always been enjoyable to me.**

the excitement of covering and writing stories, doing interviews, being at crime scenes and accidents, hanging around firefighters and police detectives and especially being recognized from television.

Some people resent fame, even after they've sought it. I've always loved it. Being *infamous* was difficult but *famous* has always been enjoyable to me.

As I won awards and recognition, I moved from Omaha to Nashville and eventually to New Orleans before heading to Detroit.

I was scheduled to start work at WXYZ-TV Channel 7 soon after my arrival, and I needed to watch the station's newscasts for a couple of days to acquaint myself with the feel, look and quality of the broadcasts so I could fit in from day one.

I was the most excited I had ever been about a television opportunity and also the most nervous. Channel 7 in Detroit would test my skills as a reporter more than any other job I'd had, even though I had about ten years of reporting experience by that point, and had already won several regional and national awards.

I was well seasoned, with good skills built upon a solid foundation of natural talent. But this job meant operating at a level that hadn't been required of me before.

It was also my first regular full-time position as an anchor.

Even though it was only the weekend anchor slot, it still meant having my name on the *marquee* and doing two newscasts each on Saturday and Sunday, plus being one of the regular fill-ins for the major weekday newscasts.

At the smaller market stations where I had crafted my reporting skills, reporters *might* be asked to deliver two stories a day. But in Detroit, reporters were routinely required to do two stories *for each newscast.*

Frank working the Democratic National Convention for WXYZ-TV Channel 7, 1996.

There was also a lot more *live* reporting; and covering "breaking news" stories in those days meant a lot more than just having a helicopter hover over a trash fire.

It meant getting to a scene where something important had actually happened, gathering as much information as possible in a matter of minutes, and then doing a "live shot" even while you were still gathering facts on the air.

As I watched the station's newscasts for those two days, I knew that I needed to hit the ground running and bring my work to a whole new level right from the start.

I initially made the empty promise to myself that I would not repeat the pattern of behavior that had threatened most of my previous positions. For a moment, I even thought my nervous excitement would be enough to scare me straight.

The long list of accomplishments and awards were telling only a portion of my resumé. Even though my talent and ability to produce extremely creative and notable work had usually been enough to make my colleagues and bosses look the other way concerning my obvious substance abuse problems, there was always a cloud, figuratively and literally hanging over my career.

> There was always a cloud, figuratively and literally hanging over my career.

By now, most of the memories have been burned up in the bonfire of brain cells destroyed in the haze of drug addiction. But I can still recall the years when extended "sick leave" and unexplained absences from work eventually led to sudden departures from TV jobs in the midst of rumors and speculation about addiction and self-destruction.

In the back of my mind, the fear that this latest opportunity in Detroit that could mean so much, might instead end just as badly, was making me nervous.

I openly showed my excitement and enthusiasm and kept my nervousness hidden under a blanket of bravado.

I was hungry for the new level of television exposure. I told myself that I could handle the job and that the nervousness would fade.

I had come to Detroit to be made into a star and I intended to carry myself like I knew I was already a star right from the beginning.

Unlike the smaller markets I had worked in, television personalities in Detroit were regarded as celebrities, and our work was truly appreciated and respected.

But having said all that, it's obvious that nowhere in my mind was I taking into account that I was a raging alcoholic and drug addict, smoking hundreds of dollars worth of cocaine a week, tied up in a brand new unwanted marriage that was certain to explode in disaster and that my entire life was built on top of a festering cesspool of unresolved issues from abandonment and abuse.

> I was a raging alcoholic and drug addict.

Not to mention the fact that I knew I was the only person available to rely on as well as the one person I absolutely could not trust—except to do the wrong thing.

Amazing how much you can do with denial.

And here's the worst part: I was already looking for a transition team.

The Transition Team

In no time at all, I was settled in and doing a standout job as an excellent reporter, a solid news anchor, and well on my way to becoming a Detroit television fixture.

But what I still desperately needed and was actively seeking was a *transition team*. Time was running out. My drug stash from New Orleans, replenished during a return trip to pick up my new wife and stepson, was running out. I needed a transition team.

The hardest adjustment for any drug addict to make during a major move is finding a transition team.

But every drug addict who has ever made a major move to a new city, a new job, a new school, any new situation where their drug setup was disrupted by a new environment or running with a new crowd has had to find a transition team.

The transition team is what I call the people a drug addict needs to identify and enlist to rebuild their network of drug users and dealers so that in their new environment they have people to buy drugs from and share drugs with.

The transition team can't be made up of just anyone. You have to have people who are in your professional, economic or social circle.

They have to be people who have as much or more to lose as you so they can be trusted. They have to be people with a vested interest in being discreet, keeping your secrets, hiding their behavior, not adding to the gossip about you and who won't turn you in if they get busted.

Here's another irony (another among the millions): you can't usually find many drug addicts with that much character.

But in high-profile public circles, discretion is valued even where integrity is not, and throughout my career, I always found that a television station was an easy place to put a transition team together.

Don't be surprised that there are drug addicts and alcoholics among the people who gather and report your nightly news. There are drug addicts and alcoholics in *every* realm of life.

> There are drug addicts and alcoholics among the people who gather and report your nightly news.

It's much more amazing in America to find someone who *is not* a drug addicted alcoholic.

Think about it, we actually import marijuana, cocaine and heroin into this country *daily* by the *ton*. Only a tiny fraction is captured by law enforcement, the rest makes it to the street and none of that gets thrown away; *it is consumed*.

We produce enough alcohol every day in this country to replace the mighty Mississippi and drink enough to drain it dry. Where do you think distillers and brewers get all those hundreds of millions of dollars they spend to sponsor sporting events on TV?

The American answer to every condition from weight loss to sore shoulders is to pop a pill. We'd rather drive to the store and get the weight loss pill we wouldn't need if we were willing to walk to the store instead. Every ache, every twinge, every pain requires a new prescription.

We'll smoke anything. We choke down the cigarettes rolled out by tobacco companies that spend millions out of the billions of dollars we pay them, to run commercials telling people not to smoke!

They not only put warnings on the side of the pack saying, "Smoking these will kill you, stupid!" They even put the same warnings on the signs advertising the special reduced price for buying a carton.

Nicotine addicts buy them anyway and then try to yell "Lawsuit!" while they're choking out their dying breath.

We are a nation of addicted smokers, tokers, snorters, sniffers, shooters, poppers and pourers.

People love to get high because they hate being sober. Sobriety is reality and reality is painful for a lot of people.

Reality is the realm of where they were raped and molested. Reality is the realm of where they were orphaned, abandoned and abused. Reality is the realm of where they were broken, beaten, divorced, fired or bankrupted. Reality is the realm of where they are unwanted or unloved. Reality is the realm of where they are rejected, unneeded and unnoticed.

Reality for many is the realm that sobriety renders unbearable. People choose intoxication because life looks better to them through distorted vision, hazy thinking, and clouded perceptions.

Reality is the realm from which people are trying to escape. Intoxication is the fastest ticket out.

But when the ticket of choice is illegal and you're in a new environment, then you need a transition team.

Let Me Give You a Hint

Building a transition team for a drug addict at a new job is a lot like a man flirting with a married woman. You pick a promising prospect, look for a few subtle signs that might indicate interest, drop a few hints and before you know it, the conversational ball is rolling right over what could've been a very sensitive subject.

The easy part is that drug addicts want to be discovered; at least by other addicts. The hard part is that no one wants to be the first to say too much too soon and wind up exposed as an addict to someone who is not.

But with some carefully placed casual comments to particular people about partying, getting trashed, or really getting messed up by some stuff that was more than you expected, you eventually get some nibbles from people who'll venture a query like…"What are you into?"

And, bam! Just like that, transition team. You tell them, they tell you, and before you know it, they're plugging you into the network of supply and demand of whatever it is that you both like.

But the harder the substance, the harder the subject is to broach. For instance, it's nothing to find out who you can go to the bar with. Nobody is hiding public consumption of alcohol, even if they're going to the bar every night after work.

When you start getting into who keeps a bottle in their desk so you can share a shot at work, that's a little harder. Going on up the ladder of difficult subjects is who has pills to pop, marijuana to sell or share, cocaine to snort and finally who's into pure rock cocaine to smoke.

There's an intoxication network for everyone, but you need a transition team to get you plugged into it. And because everybody's not into *every thing*, sometimes you might need people on a couple of teams to hook you up with different networks.

In television, particularly television news, whether it involves on-air talent or behind-the-scenes production people, one factor puts everyone on equal footing: discovery is deadly and so discretion is the better part of continued employment. And when it comes to on-air personalities, images and reputations take years to build and only seconds to destroy.

> Images and reputations take years to build and only seconds to destroy.

Since everyone's living at the station is riding on the same reputations, even when it is widely known which anchor chairs are filled with addicts, most people will help cover up even what they can't condone.

Still, the buying, selling and using of drugs at work is risky and reckless to say the least; especially when your job is performed with a high profile in the public eye under an intense spotlight.

When your transition team is at your place of employment and your supply network is made up of co-workers and colleagues, it is an indication that you are a particularly desperate and damaged individual.

When someone is willing to put everything they have, everything they are, and everything they've worked their entire careers for in the toilet and live with their fingers jiggling the handle, that is someone for whom the "high life" has taken precedence over real life.

Within weeks of arriving at Channel 7, the greatest, biggest and most important opportunity of my life, I found out that's exactly who I was.

When I arrived in Detroit on October 9, 1990 I had a date with death. I had no idea it was looming on the horizon. And I had no idea that there was something deep inside of me that was going to make sure I didn't miss it.

Up in Smoke

[W]hereas you do not know what will happen tomorrow. For what is your life? It is even a vapor that appears for a little time and then vanishes away (James 4:14).

I'd once promised that if the indulgence of any drug would cost my life, then so be it and that I would thank whatever the substance was for the sweet release. I had forgotten my promise of thanks by the first time I was actually dying from an overdose more than twenty years later. There would've been so many drugs to thank had I remembered my childhood pledge to express my gratitude.

The champagne flowing from the bottle that had fallen from my limp hand onto the concrete patio where I was crumpled and slumped down into a deck chair was certainly due an honorable mention.

And of course the quarter ounce of marijuana I had consumed within the last couple of hours no doubt was playing a starring role in my untimely demise and also deserved a nod; at least beyond the nod I was giving to the pitch black night as my head slumped over allowing a drool of foamy white spittle to run down my chin.

> Cocaine is what the coroner would've had to list on my certificate as the main contributor to my death.

But the greatest applause would undoubtedly have to go to the massive amount of cocaine that I had been steadily consuming for several hours. By snorting it, smoking it, rolling it up with the marijuana and toking it, pouring it into the champagne and drinking it, and finally in a last desperate attempt to consume all of it, just licking it off my fingers and literally eating it, I think I made sure that cocaine is what the coroner would've had to list on my certificate as the main contributor to my death.

One of the last thoughts to flow through my mind, before the blood stopped flowing through my heart was that I must be hallucinating; that stars don't actually shoot and dance across the sky, at least not all at once, and certainly not to music.

I'd been a stone-cold cocaine junkie crack-head for about twenty years at that point, but it was the first time I'd been that "high" and that scared.

As I stared up through the pitch black darkness into Nassau's Bahamian sky, the stars were shooting across it and dancing to music. At first I was fascinated. And then it occurred to me that stars can't dance, that I wasn't playing any music and no matter how hard I squinted my eyes or shook my head, I couldn't make it stop.

> This, I realized, was where I was going to die.

And then I got scared; very, very scared.

But the fear didn't last long and soon gave way to resignation. This, I realized, was where I was going to die.

Looking back I can find a sadly amusing irony in dying in the one spot where I thought I had found my life and all the peace and happiness life can hold as its ultimate promise.

This wonderful spot on this beautiful island had become a

haven for the healing of my broken heart. In that moment, slumped over in the chair, I was facing the ocean which I had stared at on many other occasions, while allowing the peace of the moments to wash over me, as the waves crashed onto the coral reef just a few feet from the patio.

The luxurious bungalow to which the patio was attached had been discovered in the relentless search for an adulterer's hideaway. It was a largely undiscovered treasure that sat right at the ocean's edge and had the patio that faced the water and a private enclosed swimming pool on the other side with the living quarters nestled between.

As my second marriage was deteriorating into my second divorce, I had begun an affair with a television colleague who was also married. It was our diligent search for a private place to hide from the public eye that brought us to Nassau and this exclusive little resort tucked away behind a marine park that was a popular tourist attraction.

As both our marriages descended past separation and into divorce, we no longer needed to hide; but as public figures, watched by millions on television every night, we still enjoyed the privacy and we began to retreat to our island getaway several times a year.

It was a dangerous enterprise.

Even though we routinely passed through Customs, had our passports inspected and often had our luggage scrutinized, it somehow still didn't really register with me that the Bahamian Islands are in a *foreign* country.

It also somehow didn't really register with me that as I routinely smuggled marijuana, cocaine and drug paraphernalia *into* that foreign country, that I was putting us both at risk and leaving our futures open to be destroyed by the harsher and less forgiving drug laws of the Bahamian government.

Not that I really would've cared.

By this time, drugs were such an integral part of my everyday existence and so woven into the fabric of my life that to go anywhere at anytime without a stash was completely out of the question, no matter what the risk or consequences.

But in many ways, Nassau itself had also become a tranquilizing intoxicant. Going there, as often as every four months or so when possible, was extremely therapeutic and a lot less dangerous than using drugs, that is, once you got past smuggling the drugs in.

In fact, it was going to the Bahamas, that truly helped me cement in my mind that not only was my drug addiction the anesthetic for my pain; it had become its own separate affliction.

> My drug addiction had become its own separate affliction.

Several times in the Bahamas I felt completely at peace. I felt whole. I felt healed. And yet, I still never wanted to feel sober.

Long, wonderful days spent sailing on catamarans across crystal clear waves of sparkling blue and green waters; lazy days spent drifting on a raft in my private pool and baking in the sun; adventurous nights spent exploring island nightspots, and tourist traps as well as little known secrets available only to the experienced visitor were nonetheless spent high on marijuana, juiced on cocaine and drunk on alcohol.

On so many occasions, I had been completely overwhelmed by the embrace of warm tropical breezes, the caress of unfiltered sun beaming from a cloudless sky, and the secure comfort of knowing that I was thousands of miles away from anything that had plagued me.

On so many occasions, the nightmares of my childhood and adult life had been washed away by daydreams driven by the peace and tranquility of hours spent staring at white and pink sandy beaches.

On so many occasions, it seemed like Heaven.

But there was *never* an occasion when I didn't still need to be high.

In the Bahamas, I discovered that even when I didn't need to be high to ease the pain of life, I still needed to get high to correct the condition of being sober. The "high life" was my life.

And now on that patio, even as in that very moment I was fulfilling my long ago and far away pledge to explore the farthest reaches of the "high," I was not doing it out of the pain and unbearable heartache I had once sought so diligently to escape.

I wasn't even doing it just to keep the pledge I had once made and long since forgotten.

I was now pushing the envelope at the farthest reaches of the "high" just because...well, just because.

The stronghold of addiction had turned my perspectives so inside out and upside down that I spoke of being sober as being "sick," getting high was getting "well," and sucking down poison was called having a "party."

In my mind happiness was getting hammered and a good day was one that could start with getting drunk.

Moods no longer mattered. By this time I was getting high on bad days as consolation, on good days as celebration. I got high when I was bored and stayed high when I was busy. I got high as the first act to welcome the morning and as the last official act that closed out the day.

The addiction from which I was dying had taken on a life of its own. And so, what was finally at this moment actually happening was always, inevitably, what was going to happen.

The private suicide party that had been in full swing hours before my companion went to bed had now continued hours after she had fallen asleep. I had started by the pool but the roar of the ocean waves crashing against the coral reef had drawn me to the patio.

> On this trip I had brought the largest amount of cocaine I had ever smuggled.

As funny as it now sounds to me, I ended up getting too high, because of my frustration over not being able to get high enough.

On this trip I had brought the largest amount of cocaine I had ever smuggled into the islands, a full ounce. A quarter of it had been "cooked" for smoking, but I hadn't brought a pipe.

I hadn't brought marijuana on this trip either because we had made friends with some natives of the island who had finally convinced me of the foolishness and needlessness of bringing marijuana *into* the Bahamas.

I already knew some of the most potent pot in the world could be found *on* the islands, it was just that until I knew someone I could trust to get it for me, I thought it less dangerous to bring my own.

I was not, however, going to acquire cocaine from anyone except my usual, trusted Detroit connection; and so risk or not, I always brought that with me.

On previous trips, snorting powdered cocaine, while not ideal, usually had to suffice. For someone who *smokes* pure cocaine though, snorting powder can be a bit of a tease. It's kind of like the difference between drinking rum in a daiquiri versus straight from the bottle.

But I always managed to bring a pure enough quality of coke that snorting it had almost as much of a punch as smoking it.

This time though I had planned to *smoke some rock* as the ultimate experience of enjoying our little getaway, but there was one major hitch. Cocaine, I could safely stash. Trust me, you don't want to know how or where, but let's just say no law enforcement officer wanted to find it *that* bad.

But there was no way I could hide a glass pipe in the same manner. This meant that I had to come to the island with cocaine that could only be smoked and without a way to smoke it.

Once there, even though marijuana could be acquired from our new friends, asking them for cocaine paraphernalia seemed too risky.

We always traveled the island by the same private taxi service and asking the driver, who had become quite acquainted with us to take me somewhere to score a "crack pipe" was also out of the question.

The other problem was that our bungalow was so remote and secluded that it was miles from any commercial area that I might walk to on my own in search of a pipe or something that I could use to make a reasonable substitution.

> Asking the driver to score a "crack pipe" was also out of the question.

And so by not thinking things through, I had put myself into the drug addict's worst nightmare scenario: I had drugs that I couldn't consume.

When I say nightmare, I don't mean figuratively. One horrible feature of the creative mind shared by every crack-head is the "pipe dream."

There are as many variations as there are imaginations, but the basic gist of them is simple: you've got a ton of rock cocaine and for some reason, you can't smoke it.

Sometimes, I would awaken in the middle of the night, drenched in a cold sweat and shaking uncontrollably after a nightmare episode in which I had a brand new pipe and fresh supply of rock, but no matter how hard I flicked my "bic" I couldn't get it to light.

Another version is that your pipe is so clogged that no matter how hard you pull on it, you can't get any smoke to come through.

No matter what the variation on the theme, the result is the same: you awaken suddenly, totally frustrated, completely strung out and with the taste of cocaine so strongly painted across your tongue that you are desperately determined in that moment to get as high as you can as soon as you are able.

Like most regular crack-heads, I had pipe dreams virtually every time I went to sleep.

For a crack-head to be looking at rock cocaine in real life and not be able to smoke it is literally a nightmare come true. But there I was. The situation seemed hopeless.

Diligently, I searched every cabinet of our bungalow and considered every container of every toiletry as a possible solution to my desperate need for a crack pipe. I had always prided myself on being the "MacGyver" of drug paraphernalia and even knew how to make a marijuana pipe from an apple. But I simply could not find the necessary elements to enable smoking that "rock."

> ## That set the stage for the beginning of the end.

It was that frustration that set the stage for the beginning of the end and put the wheels in motion that would later help roll me away on a stretcher while paramedics pumped my chest.

With no other alternative, I began crushing and mashing

the "rock" with a spoon and using a razor blade to then chop it into the finest powder that I was able, so that I could mingle it with the marijuana and try to roll it up and smoke it in the "joints."

It was a huge mistake.

If you're ever looking for the ultimate "crack-head's conundrum" to stump the average pipe junkie, try this question: "Which is better (or worse, depending upon your perspective), to have "rock" cocaine and try to not start smoking it at all, or to start smoking it and not be able to smoke enough to get a *good* hit?"

Wow. That's a toughie.

Actually though, I think it would have been better to face the frustration of trying not to smoke it than dealing with the absolute nightmarish aggravation of not being able to smoke *enough* of it.

The chemistry of cocaine and its effect on the brain is such that there is never a hit as good as the first one. You also can't stop the brain from trying to "chase" the *first* hit with every *subsequent* hit in a futile attempt to match it or top it.

What this means is that the more you smoke, the more you try to smoke. The "hits" have to not only keep coming, but they have to get bigger, and stronger as you try to suck down more and more of the drug. The irony is that the more you smoke, the harder you make it to recapture that first feeling or "rush."

That's because the first rush was the effect of a wave of cocaine hitting a sober system. With each subsequent "hit," you are that much more intoxicated and that much less able to really "shock" your system.

If you could stop smoking just long enough to "come down" and sober up a bit, you could get that "first hit" feeling again. But there's another of the countless ironies of being a drug addict; once you start smoking cocaine, your consumption only grows more frantic and frenzied until it's all gone.

That night, with no way to smoke it other than rolled up in the marijuana, I never really did get a *good* "hit," only a lot of frustration. Before I knew it, I had smoked all the marijuana, trying to smoke the cocaine and now I couldn't even continue to smoke it that way.

Since "cooked" cocaine can't be snorted, I was left with trying to sustain my high with the powdered cocaine, which actually made up the vast majority of what I had.

But *snorting* a lot of coke can't compare with *smoking* even a little, and so before I knew it, I was trying to maintain a *smoking* level buzz without actually having a way to consume the coke at that level.

And thus, in addition to snorting as much as possible, I was also pouring cocaine into the champagne bottle and drinking it, re-rolling the marijuana butts ("roaches," ok?) with more cocaine and toking it, re-rolling tobacco from my cigarettes in reefer paper with cocaine and smoking it, and finally just smearing so much of it around my teeth and gums and licking it off my fingers that I was actually eating it.

> I was also pouring cocaine into the champagne.

That brings us back to the patio and the white frothy spittle foaming out of my mouth.

But actually, let's stop at a point prior to that moment because I'd really like to share with you the details of one of the most terrifying times of my life.

Looking back, I don't think I've ever been as scared as I was in those moments when I looked up into the sky and saw the stars begin to dance.

The Fear Factor

The terror eventually gave way to resignation—recognition of the fact that I was going to die. But before I reached the end of the road to resignation, I traveled a path through a territory that I had never seen before.

It was fear. Not just any fear, but a gripping, shuddering, all encompassing fear that rattled me to the bone and sent waves of anxiety through my mind and body that were much like the waves crashing in the darkness upon the reef in front of me.

> Terror eventually gave way to resignation that I was going to die.

It wasn't that I was afraid of *dying* but more that I was afraid of *the way* I was dying.

Under the influence of hallucinogens like mescaline and LSD at other times in my life, I had experienced seeing things that were not there, observing events that were actually not happening and being fooled by drug induced illusions of an overly intoxicated and polluted mind.

But cocaine is not usually hallucinogenic, at least it had never been for me, and I knew that what my mind believed my eyes were seeing, was the result of being thrust into a new realm, a new level of over-intoxication that I had never visited before.

At this point, I had been steadily ingesting tobacco, marijuana, alcohol and massive amounts of cocaine for at least five hours. My heart was racing, my pulse was pounding and my head felt swollen and "fat."

I was flushed and hot and even though nothing was between my skin and the mild tropical evening breeze but a t-shirt and shorts, I was sweating profusely.

I remember my ears were ringing with a steady tone that was peppered with the rapid beats from my overworked heart.

The heart really takes a beating (no pun intended) under the influence of cocaine. While the drug increases the blood pressure by racing the heart, it simultaneously serves to constrict the blood vessels, restricting their flow.

You end up with a heart racing faster and faster as it tries harder and harder to pump more and more blood through vessels that are shrinking tighter and tighter. It includes all the ingredients of a recipe for death.

Since the gradually increasing effects of snorting cocaine are more slowly realized than the instantaneous effects of smoking it, I had put way too much into my system by the time I recognized it; combined with all the nicotine, alcohol and marijuana.

All of which became undeniably evident when I began to stare up into the night sky and witnessed what appeared to be stars actually moving. But not all at once.

Eventually they all danced. But at first, one star just moved. I was looking into the sky when I noticed the star "scoot" from one spot to another.

That's strange, I thought. And I stared—first at the spot the star moved to and then back at the spot where it had been. And as I stared, it moved again. It *was* happening and yet, I knew it could *not* be happening.

I had never seen such a thing. It was an illusion, a hallucination, a wayward drug-induced vision and yet it was so real, so believably real. I squinted and rubbed my eyes and shook my head but that star continued to "flit" from one spot to another and then other stars began do the same thing.

I was scared; terrified; frightened beyond any boundary I had ever previously crossed. I was coming to the realization that for me to see what my mind thought I was seeing meant that my head must be about to explode.

> I was scared; terrified; frightened beyond any boundary I had ever previously crossed.

And that's when the music started. This terrifying delusion was suddenly being accompanied by the symphonic sound of an orchestra in my imagination that played a ballet to which all the stars in my range of vision began to dance.

I was captivated; I was enthralled. Hundreds of stars

were moving back and forth across the sky, forming patterns and shapes, swirling and spinning, and then bursting apart like dazzling fireworks before coming together again into new patterns.

I was mesmerized and I was afraid. Again, not so much because I knew or sensed that it was the end of my life, but more because of the way my life was ending.

I figured I was seconds away from my heart seizing into arrest, or my brain exploding from a stroke or a combination of the two. But whatever was about to happen, I knew it was causing me to see something so vivid, so incredibly, undeniably real that at the same time, obviously could not be truly happening.

And that is what frightened me. As my brain was being pushed into this previously unknown region, what else might I see or feel on this path leading inevitably to my demise?

And then just like that, the fear subsided. The terror and anxiety that gripped me mentally and physically; that caused my head to roar and my body to quake; that washed over me in wave after crashing wave, subsided and then ceased.

I slumped back in my chair, fixed my gaze on the sky and continued to watch the "show."

In the absence of fear, I was resigned to yet another in a long string of ironies: that after all the pain, heartache, destruction, abuse and death I had suffered, endured and been shaped and shifted by; my life was ending at what was to that point the *best time* of my life, in the most peaceful place I'd ever visited, just a few feet away from a woman who thought I was her future and had no idea that death was sitting on her patio.

A Rude Awakening

Cardiac arrest is not easily reversed and the efforts required to bring someone back from death are startling, to say the least, particularly to the guest of honor.

I mean, there I was one minute, minding my own business, slumped over dead in a patio chair above a pool of my own urine with a thick white foam of cocaine-laced spittle drooling from my mouth; not breathing, heart not beating; and then, seemingly the next minute, I'm in the back of an ambulance being assaulted by paramedics pumping my chest and shouting at me and each other in thick Bahamian accents.

> The efforts required to bring someone back from death are startling.

Talk about a rude awakening.

I was dazed, confused and quite disoriented. But I was also relieved; at least about being alive. I was scared about what I might face at the hospital and eventually perhaps even from the police.

My companion had awakened, apparently very soon after I stopped breathing, discovered me on the patio, quickly assessed the desperate nature of the situation and called for the ambulance.

Her actions were heroic indeed. Not only the measures she took to try and save my life before help arrived, but even being willing to be connected to a fatal overdose of narcotics that had been smuggled into a foreign country.

Saving my life could've cost her freedom.

Before the ambulance and police arrived, she had cleaned up all the drugs, gathered all the paraphernalia and disposed of every incriminating thing she could find.

As the ambulance, with the paramedics quickly but efficiently working on me sped on its way to the emergency room of the hospital where I would be stabilized, evaluated, put back on my feet and eventually released, I remember thinking *I hope she hid that cocaine in a safe place.* After all, I thought, *that stuff was good.*

> I hope she hid that cocaine in a safe place.

CHAPTER FIVE

A CERTAIN MAN IS SICK

Now a certain *man* was sick, Lazarus of Bethany,
the town of Mary and her sister Martha
(John 11:1).

T here are so many wonderful parallels and amazing comparisons between the Biblical account of Lazarus being raised from the dead and my restoration and redemption in Christ that my testimony of resurrection can actually be told through much of what is recorded in the eleventh chapter of the gospel of John.

Some would call the description of what happened to Lazarus a Bible story. I always use the word *account* when speaking of the truths recorded in the Scriptures rather than *story*. The word *story* tends to leave the door open for these truths to be regarded as myths, fables or legends.

Biblical truths are not mere stories, but historical accounts of actual events recorded for the purpose of revealing the awesome power and love of our holy and righteous God. These accounts are not just to be read and left as words on a page, but to be seen and lived in the mind as if you are really there.

I'd like you to consider the elements of the testimony of

my life in parallel with the account of Lazarus and all the while, truly imagine the experiences with me. If you'll put yourself right there with me, I *guarantee* you'll see the glory of God!

The name Lazarus is known the world over. He is the iconic personification of the idea of *anyone* or *anything* being "raised from the dead." But the Bible records the actual event, the actual occurrence, the actual day that a real man named Lazarus from the real town of Bethany was actually raised from the dead.

While Lazarus' name is of great renown, most don't really know the awesome and intricate details of what came to pass before, during and after this miraculous event. It is such a marvelous account that it deserves careful inspection and understanding. And when you appreciate the marvel of Lazarus, you'll fully appreciate what the Lord did for me.

> Lazarus is the iconic personification of *anyone* being "raised from the dead."

Now a certain man *was* sick, Lazarus of Bethany, the town of Mary and her sister Martha. It was *that* Mary who anointed the Lord with fragrant oil and wiped His feet with her hair, whose brother Lazarus was sick. Therefore the sisters sent to Him, saying, "Lord, behold, he whom You love is sick." When Jesus heard *that*, He said, "This sickness is not unto death, but for the glory of God, that the Son of God may be glorified through it." Now Jesus loved Martha and her sister and Lazarus. So, when He heard that he was sick, He stayed two more days in the place where He was (John 11:1–6).

It's not clear whether his family or friends knew exactly what was ailing Lazarus, but they obviously knew his situation was desperate and his sisters knew the only one who could help was Jesus; and so they sent Him a message.

> The only one who could help was Jesus.

The Lord Jesus, however, knew exactly how sick Lazarus was and that while his sickness would indeed kill him; it would ultimately provide the opportunity for an amazing miracle that would bring glory to God.

The Lord Jesus Christ Loves Frank Turner

By January of 1998 there were a lot of people sending petitions to Jesus to come and help Frank Turner. They were not my relatives, but most did consider me part of their families. They were television viewers who, for eight years, had watched my rise to prominence as I became co-anchor of the highest rated 5:00 newscast in Detroit, Michigan.

The move from New Orleans in 1990 to this major television market to take the job at WXYZ-TV Channel 7 was the best of my broadcasting career.

Within a few years, I had distinguished myself as an exceptional anchor and reporter, won several local and regional awards including a coveted *Emmy* and was marked as a rising star. In 1995, during a major talent shuffle at the station, I was promoted to the weeknight anchor position at 5:00 in the evening.

I had been gifted with a quick wit, a warm smile and the ability to project an energetic personality. I made an immediate and strong connection with our viewers. They adopted me into their families, and through their televisions, invited me into their homes every day.

The newscast, which some industry insiders thought would suffer from the sudden talent shake-up at the station, almost immediately regained its number one position and stayed there.

However, less than three years after becoming the 5:00 anchor, my professional life began to publicly fall apart. My personal life had actually been a disaster for a long time, yet I had managed to hide it. But by January of 1998 it was obvious to everyone that Frank Turner was "sick." I was suspended from my job and had disappeared from the airwaves.

> I was suspended from my job and disappeared from the airwaves.

As in the case of Lazarus, no one knew exactly what was wrong. But in my case, there were rumors. The local newspapers reported that a former girlfriend was suing me claiming that I had been using our credit cards to call phone sex lines. And it was also being rumored that the mess my life and career had degenerated into was the result of drug addiction.

Anchors of nightly major market television newscasts don't disappear quietly. My absence was notable and my personal and professional problems were reported in the daily newspapers, discussed on talk-radio programs and covered by my competitors on other stations.

As with Lazarus, those who loved me; those who considered me a member of their family, turned to Jesus on my behalf. Many of the people praying for me—thousands—were viewers, and over the years I had met a lot of them in person. But there were also hundreds of thousands of people I'd neither met nor who had even watched me on television, who were led to pray on my behalf.

> There were also hundreds of thousands of people I'd neither met nor who had even watched me on television, who were led to pray on my behalf.

They knew something that I didn't. They knew that Jesus loved me. I didn't even know what that meant at the time.

These praying people also knew that God's love was a gift of grace. I didn't know what that meant either.

At that time, with my professional life being destroyed, my personal life in ruins and all of the gifts and opportunities I'd been given going to waste, I felt so ashamed; so unworthy;

so unloved and unlovable that the idea of receiving something by *grace* felt completely foreign and incomprehensible. And yet by definition, grace is something that cannot be earned or deserved.

I felt utterly alone and I wanted to die. Actually I did—three times.

But staying dead was not God's plan for me. Instead, He had already decided to use my sickness and death in the same way He used that of Lazarus.

God would use my sickness and the prayers on my behalf to create a miraculous bond between Himself and me and the people praying for me. That bond would be a miracle that would also bring glory to God the Father and to the Lord Jesus Christ.

And in my case, every single detail of how I came to be crippled by addiction and shame, paralyzed by misery and depression, and destroyed by abandonment and death would become part of a testimony to God's unlimited gift of grace.

God's plan was for the utter destruction of my life to be chronicled from tragic beginning to miraculous and glorious end.

> God's plan for bringing believers to Christ was already in motion.

And even as bad became worse, the plan to bring glory to God while bringing believers to Christ was already in motion

When Jesus received the petition on Lazarus' behalf, his answer to it was that Lazarus' sickness would not ultimately result in death, but that He and the Father would be glorified.

In my case, I certainly did not know that what was to

happen to me, even though death seemed the only escape, would lead to life and the glory of God.

Jesus Knows What the Sickness Is

I didn't know it at the time but we have the assurance that the Lord Jesus always knows exactly what our problems are. No matter what we are going through, no matter how desperate the situation seems, Jesus knows exactly what is happening and has a plan to use it for our good and His glory.

I can assure you right now, that no matter what you are going through, the Lord Jesus knows about it, has a plan to see you through it, and plans to get His glory on the other side of it, when you tell the testimony of how He brought you out of it.

> No matter what we are going through, Jesus knows what is happening.

That is, if at any point, no matter if it seems far too late, you will call on Him.

When the Lord was told of Lazarus' sickness, He told the disciples with Him that Lazarus' sickness would not end with a bad result, but with God receiving glory. And unlike everyone else who was gripped with concern, fear and uncertainty, Jesus knew exactly what was making Lazarus sick.

What the others with Him also did not know is that by the time Jesus was receiving this message, Lazarus had already died! The timing was such that even as Jesus was saying his sickness would not *end* in death, Lazarus *was* dead.

The Lord was saying that the glory of God would be seen, not by saving Lazarus from the fatal consequences of his sickness, but by allowing the situation to take its course and then raising Lazarus from the grave.

Likewise, even as prayers and petitions were being offered for me, Jesus knew exactly what was making me sick and that my death professionally and physically was just as inevitable. But no one else knew He was going to let my sickness run its course and then snatch me back from the jaws of death.

> He was going to snatch me back from the jaws of death.

Only Jesus Could Save Me

Only the Lord could declare that the sickness which has already killed a man is "...not unto death..." Jesus can make that declaration because He *is* life. This makes the next development in the cases of Lazarus *and* me even more amazing.

Now Jesus loved Martha and her sister and Lazarus. So, when He heard that he was sick, He stayed two more days in the place where He was (John 11:5–6).

In spite of the urgent petition to come to Lazarus' aid,

Jesus decided to remain where He was for another two days!

Remember, the Lord had promised to use this situation for the glory of God. Jesus' delay is to assure that the miracle of what He will do with Lazarus cannot be attributed to anything or anyone else. At this point the situation is not yet desperate and hopeless enough.

Jesus planned to arrive only after Lazarus had lain in his tomb for four days! This means that Lazarus must have died the same day Jesus received the notice to come help him. It would have been customary to bury him that same day. Jesus then *waits* two additional days, so that after He takes a day to journey to Bethany from "beyond Jordan" (John 10:40) where He was, He would arrive on the fourth day Lazarus was in the grave.

And the delay, John tells us is *because of Jesus' love for Lazarus, Martha and Mary.* Jesus' waiting until exactly the appointed time will ultimately be for their good and God's glory!

But imagine how strange it must have seemed to those who were with the Lord to see Him delay in answering such an urgent petition. They certainly did not understand that *only by waiting* could every doubt be removed that God alone has the power over life and death and that Jesus is the Son of God.

It was common, among doubters and detractors of Christ who could not discount His miracles, to attribute them to the devil. Some historians have also recorded a superstition among the Jews of that time that the soul hovered near a dead body for three days hoping to reenter it.

But after four days, no one would be able to discount the miracle of raising Lazarus; no one would be able to attribute it to any superstitious notion. The praise and the glory would have to be given to God!

In that same way, it must have seemed strange to those praying for me so fervently that Jesus delayed in coming to the rescue even as my condition grew much worse. And in effect, by the time the prayers and petitions reached Jesus on my behalf, I was as good as dead already.

Less than four months after my January suspension, the station fired me. It wasn't a quiet, hardly noticed firing. It was a public, painful, excruciatingly embarrassing and debilitating firing. It was a widely reported and much talked about firing. It was a front-page-of-the-newspaper, hot-topic on talk radio, talk-about-it at-the water cooler firing.

It was an end-of-the-line, my-life-is-over, curl-up-and-die kind of firing.

There I was, one of the most recognized faces and well known television personalities in Detroit, the number one 5:00 news anchor in the market, the man who had everything; suddenly disgraced, exposed, fired.

The false allegations of credit card fraud in a lawsuit filed against me by my former girlfriend, *though untrue*, were exposing the most humiliating details of my personal life including a deep involvement with phone sex prostitutes whose calls had been charged to the joint credit cards in question.

Every development of my crumbling life was being

reported daily. And revelations about my drug addiction, kept hidden in the shadows for so many years, were now coming to light.

Still, no one could have yet fathomed the depth to which addiction had mired me in the sludge of a destroyed life. But I feared it was only a matter of time before some of the colleagues and co-workers with whom I had been buying and consuming drugs came forward to confirm the worst of the rumors as truth.

In fact, given the extent to which I was involved in the drug trafficking and use within the station, it was actually amazing that only my situation was being exposed. And no doubt, the others must have feared that my exposure could cost their careers as well.

Like many with far too much to lose, I had been reckless beyond reason. I regularly smoked marijuana in the news trucks even while on assignment. And because the drug connection who supplied me and others at the station was also a news photographer with whom I routinely covered stories, we sometimes made pick ups and deliveries in the news trucks!

> We sometimes made pick ups and deliveries in the news trucks!

At this point, the detailed revelation that each week I was consistently smoking up to an ounce of high-grade marijuana from my connection at work had not yet come to light; but because the secret involved so many other people both inside and outside the station, I was afraid it would at any moment.

All of this was hanging over my head along with the burden of the massive amounts of pure cocaine I was chronically consuming for periods of five to six days at a time without food or water, without rest or sleep, without ceasing and sometimes without even knowing how much time had passed.

> The situation was still not yet desperate and hopeless enough for His intervention.

What *was* being reported, however, was gruesome enough.

And yet, the Lord waited. At that point the situation was still not yet desperate and hopeless enough for His intervention.

Jesus intended to come to my rescue only after my situation had deteriorated and stunk as much as Lazarus had begun to in the grave.

It's common in our society to see and hear reports of people "recovering" from various addictions and rebounding from incredibly public and embarrassing setbacks.

There is even a widely circulated superstition that through the power of "positive thinking," one can induce a kind of self hypnosis and transform oneself into a better person.

But after my life finally exploded and burned, no one could discount the miracle of Christ in delivering me from death or attribute His saving grace or the healing of my body to any superstitious notion of self transformation.

Only after the stone was rolled away from Lazarus' tomb and the fullness of the stench of death from within was revealed, did it become abundantly clear that he was resurrected by a work only Christ could do.

And after every dark detail of my life is uncovered, and the stench of death is revealed, after every deep-seated, heart-wrenching wound is made undeniably evident, it will be clear that only Jesus could be responsible for what happened next to Frank Turner.

> Only Jesus could be responsible for what happened next to Frank Turner.

When the Stone Is Rolled Away

Then Jesus, again groaning in Himself, came to the tomb. It was a cave, and a stone lay against it. Jesus said, "Take away the stone" (John 11:38–39).

There was a powerful stench building in that cave and Jesus wanted it discovered. There was a dead man rotting in that tomb and Jesus wanted him exposed. The glory of God was lingering just behind that wall of rock and now it was time for the Lord Jesus to allow it to be revealed.

After four days in the grave, Lazarus had an odor that screamed death, but now he had a Savior who was going to speak life. Yet before the dead could be called to life, the death had to be verified, the stench had to be released and so the stone had to be rolled away.

No one wanted what had been hidden to be revealed, no

one wanted what lingered in the shadows to be given light, no one wanted what was sealed up in that tomb to be loosed. But for the power of the miraculous to be believed, the odor of the hopelessness had to be exposed.

Jesus had allowed the death to take place, the days to pass, and the decomposition to continue so that the stench would build for exactly this moment. Only when the world was able to smell how bad the situation was, would they fully understand and believe how good God is.

> Nothing *confirms* death like the *smell* of death.

Soon, a man who once was dead would come walking out of that grave. Jesus could not leave even the slightest *hint* of doubt that Lazarus was not only dead, but rotting away.

Nothing *confirms* death like the *smell* of death.

When that stone was rolled away, the doubt had to roll away with it.

> Jesus said to her, "Did I not say to you that if you would believe you would see the glory of God?" Then they took away the stone *from the place* where the dead man was lying. And Jesus lifted up *His* eyes and said, "Father, I thank You that You have heard Me" (John 11:40–41).

If they would believe, they would see the glory of God. They would have to believe that Jesus was not too late, but right on time. They would have to believe that no case is beyond His control, no situation beyond His repair and no hopelessness beyond His help. If they would believe that Jesus Christ is the *Son* of God they would see the *glory* of God.

> Jesus was inviting everyone to take a deep breath and keep their eyes on the tomb.

It has long been said that "seeing is believing." But it has been proven that the sense of smell is the most powerful and provocative of the senses and the one to which most of our memories are connected.

So as the stone was about to be rolled away, Jesus was inviting everyone to take a deep breath and keep their eyes on that tomb.

By This Time Frank Stinketh

There was definitely a stench building around Frank Turner and the Lord wanted it discovered. A walking dead man, I was increasingly holed up in the "tomb" I had made of my condo, but the Lord wanted me exposed. The glory of God was lingering just behind the door of my home and the time had come; the horribly painful time; the unbelievably embarrassing time; the crushing, crippling, devastating time for the Lord Jesus to allow it to be revealed.

Remember, nothing *confirms* death like the *smell* of death and there was an odor emanating from my life that was more than the aroma of unemployment.

The details of my professional "demise" were odorous indeed but the stench had a more stagnant quality. It was clear that the odor from my "tomb" had a deeper origin than what could be seen on the surface. It was also evident that what had been festering in my heart and mind had been buried for longer than anyone had imagined.

When the stone was rolled away to expose the pain and heartache, the frailties and failures, the desperation and destruction and the depression and anxiety, it became clear that there was so much more hiding in the shadows of my tomb than could be immediately discerned on the first whiff.

> Then they took away the stone *from the place* where the dead man was lying. And Jesus lifted up *His* eyes and said, "Father, I thank You that You have heard Me. And I know that You always hear Me, but because of the people who are standing by I said *this*, that they may believe that You sent Me" (John 11:41–42).

What happened next in Bethany is one of the richest experiences of all the Bible's accounts, and to fully understand it you have to actually put yourself at the scene.

You have to imagine you are standing there outside the tomb of Lazarus. You have to see the stone being rolled away *while* you are hearing the Lord Jesus thank His Heavenly Father for having already heard His petition on Lazarus' behalf.

You have to realize that as the *fullness of the stench of death* from the tomb is reaching your nostrils, *the breath of life* has already been blown into Lazarus' lungs.

Jesus is thanking His Father for hearing and answering the request on Lazarus' behalf, and He is only *saying* it out loud for the benefit of those standing at the tomb.

Jesus will call Lazarus to come out, but God has already raised him up. By the time the answer to Jesus' petition is revealed, it had already been heard and handled in the secret recesses of the tomb.

Raising Lazarus from the dead has been for God's glory. Doing it publicly is for our good; *so that we may believe*.

And so the moment the Savior had planned has arrived. The death He had allowed is being reversed. The man in the tomb is making his way toward the entrance and is about to emerge as the evidence of the power and glory of God.

But all that the crowd was about to *see* would only make sense in the light of what they had already *heard*. The crowd has already heard the Lord thank His Father for hearing His request and now they are about to see what that request has produced.

> Now when He had said these things, He cried
> with a loud voice, "Lazarus, come forth!" And
> he who had died came out bound hand and foot
> with grave clothes, and his face was wrapped
> with a cloth. Jesus said to them, "Loose him,

and let him go" (John 11:43–44).

As Lazarus emerges from the tomb, the *people of God* are standing at the crossroads where the *plan of God* and the *purpose of God* are coming together.

Lazarus' death was not to be prevented, but to be reversed.

The stench from his tomb was not to be hidden, but to be exposed.

And his call to life was not to be ignored, but to be answered; all to the glory of God and all for the good of everyone present and everyone who has learned of it since.

Can you see it? Can you imagine the splendor of this momentous occasion in history?

Right there at the tomb of a dead man, whose decomposing body has left a smell still lingering in your nostrils is the proof that Jesus is Lord, that God the Father has sent Him and that He *is* the life.

And the most wondrous part of seeing Lazarus standing there whole, fresh and alive, is the knowledge of what had formerly been hidden in the dark recesses of death before the stone was rolled away.

> Death was not to be prevented, but to be reversed.

In much the same way, here I am; called to life from death. You are here also; called to the crossroads where *the plan of God* and the *purpose of God* in my life are meeting. And like Lazarus, only the revelation of what had been hidden in the dark recesses of death before the stone was rolled away can prove the absolute wonder of me being made whole, fresh and alive.

To what illness Lazarus succumbed we cannot know until we get to Heaven and ask him.

As for what caused the death of Frank Turner, that can be told now.

What caused the death of Frank Turner, that can be told now.

CHAPTER SIX

YOU TALKIN' TO ME?

The Mighty One, God the LORD,
Has spoken and called the earth
From the rising of the sun
to its going down
(Psalm 50:1).

Suspended, fired, sued and suicidal. The house of cards had finally crumbled. The pain I couldn't endure, the addiction I couldn't break, the life I couldn't lead; the whole thing had finally crashed and burned.

My second overdose heart attack was just behind me and a second bankruptcy was just ahead.

A toxic mixture of the truth, lies, speculation and rumor was being used to paint a picture of me across the front pages of the local papers.

I had lawyers I'd stopped listening to, court appearances I couldn't keep and a world I could no longer bear to witness; so I closed the blinds, turned off the phones, grabbed that pipe and decided to finally smoke myself to death.

Suspended, fired, sued, and suicidal. The house of cards had finally crumbled.

Three or four days into the largest single stash of cocaine

I'd ever tried to consume in one sitting, I heard a voice calling my name and producing what seemed like a cavernous echo inside my head.

It wasn't dancing stars, but I dismissed it as the initial hallucinations of the oncoming stroke that would finally set me free from the misery I'd made of my life...until...snap! I was stone cold sober.

Stone cold sober. In one instant I went from a blazing high that had taken at least three days to achieve, to being stone cold sober.

If you've ever been intoxicated, imagine being as drunk or as high or as zonked as you've ever been and in one instant, suddenly, in the snap of your fingers being stone cold sober.

If you've ever flown in an airliner, imagine taking off and ascending, climbing to a cruising altitude of 40,000 feet and then...snap! Suddenly you find yourself back on the tarmac at the airport.

In one split second, I fell from stoned out of my mind to stone cold sober.

I grabbed the spoon I was using to scoop up some of the rocks of cocaine I had piled up on the plate in front of me, filled the bowl of the pipe, put the blue flame of the butane torch I was using up to the bowl, and began to draw the smoke in as hard as I could.

The hazy grayish white smoke first filled the bowl, then filled my lungs and then filled the air as I exhaled deeply after holding it in as long as I could.

Nothing. *Not a thing.* In one hit, I had inhaled more than most crack-heads smoke in a week. It was some of the freshest, purest, most potent cocaine I had ever acquired, and I had just filled my lungs to capacity with what should have been blasting my brain with chemical warfare and yet…nothing.

Stone cold sober. And then again I heard the voice, in that cavernous echo, calling my name from inside my head. "Frank."

I knew in that moment that I was in the manifest presence of God and He was talking to me.

> I knew in that moment that I was in the manifest presence of God.

It was strange to me, as I realized in one of the ten thousand thoughts suddenly racing though my mind, that I was neither afraid, nor ashamed.

I was standing there, half naked, bathed in the sweat that just moments earlier was dripping from my pores as my pounding cocaine-fueled heart was beating hard enough to be seen through my chest, with my skin again coated in that familiar corrosive cocaine residue.

I was looking down at the familiar collection of hardcore pornography used to satisfy my molestation-induced and drug-heightened obsessions.

I was holding a glass pipe with the half melted syrup of pure cocaine dripping down the stem from the filled overheated bowl.

And all this while the manifest presence of God was filling my room. It was a moment that one might expect to be followed by the sizzle of a lightning bolt that would burn me to a crisp and leave me heaped into a pile of ashes.

And yet, I felt neither shame nor fear. I think, for the first time since my mother had last held me in her arms, I felt...safe.

> For the first time since my mother had last held me in her arms I felt...safe.

I didn't assume I was going to be helped, but I knew I wasn't going to be hurt.

Also in that split second I knew two things for a certainty: I knew this *was* God whose presence I felt and I knew that I had never met Him before.

It became abundantly clear to me in that moment that the only god I had ever known was the god of my imagination; the god I made up to suit my own needs.

Like most people I knew, I had invented a god in my mind who understood me, who loved me, but who placed no requirements on me to change.

My imaginary god understood and accepted my addiction as an uncontrollable problem which he, like I, was powerless to solve.

And my imaginary god could be served in whatever way I chose, if ever I decided to give him any consideration at all.

I knew for a certainty that this God calling my name was not *that* god.

"Yes," I answered—the pipe in my hand already heading toward my mouth as my arm habitually began to raise it toward my lips.

"Go ahead. Try again," He said.

I lifted the torch, still burning from its resting place on the nightstand and placed the white tip of the blue flame to the bowl of the pipe. More smoke. Still nothing.

"Now listen," He said.

I stood there completely still; staring straight ahead like a little boy caught red-handed holding something I had been told not to touch. Again, not afraid or ashamed, but not sure what to do next. I was overwhelmed by the peace of His presence. It was nothing like I'd imagined His presence would be.

I also remember considering how strange it was to hear this voice and hearing it in my head expressing thoughts I wasn't thinking.

"It is time for this to stop," He said. "Flush all the drugs down the toilet. Throw everything else away. Clean up the mess."

"I can't," I answered. I didn't mean I wouldn't, I just meant I wasn't able to on my own. I thought this was finally my moment of release; I had no intention of responding with disobedience. What I needed was empowerment.

"Stop this now and come with Me," was His only response.

Now I was afraid. I suddenly felt the weight of an ultimatum I could not meet on my own.

I remember thinking that I could not believe I was rejecting God. It wasn't by choice, but choosing Him was beyond my ability. He was my choice, but the drug had me bound. If only

I was free I would run to do as He asked.

I wanted to beg for His help and plead for His mercy. I wanted to cry out and fall to my knees sobbing and begging to be free to do as He wanted.

But instead of a scream, I only managed to mumble another muffled, "I can't."

"You're already dead," He said next. "Your heart exploded four hours ago. It is only beating now because I am holding it in My hand. Choose Me or choose that. I won't ask you again."

The sobbing I'd been longing to have burst forth from my lips now rushed out in a flood of anguish, frustration and fear.

"I can't, I can't, I can't!" I cried. I wanted to say so much more, but that's all I could manage to utter as I wept uncontrollably.

Then as suddenly as His presence had been manifest, it was gone and I was alone. Not alone as I had been before, but an unimaginable, supernatural aloneness unlike anything I had ever experienced. It was, in that moment, as if God had completely withdrawn His presence from my apartment and created a divine vacuum of His absence.

If hell is to be the torment of the eternal separation from the presence of God, then I can say that in that moment, my apartment became the headquarters of hell.

As tangibly as I had felt His presence, I could even more tangibly feel His absence. I knew then that He had always previously been with me, around me, in me. I knew that He had been shielding me, protecting me, watching me and loving me.

I became acutely aware that the God I didn't know had always known and been with me, because by contrast in this moment, He was gone.

He allowed me to know exactly what it would be like to suffer the consequences of rejecting Him. It was an emptiness words cannot describe. It was an aloneness that cannot be fathomed without being personally felt.

Until now I'd only ever told a handful of people about this, including Nicky after she became my wife. I struggled with whether to put this in print. I know doubt, debate, scorn and ridicule will result. There will be those who will denounce me as a liar, people who will write it off as a figment of my imagination…so be it. As John the Apostle wrote, I have the witness in myself.

> It was an aloneness that cannot be fathomed without being personally felt.

There will be theologians who'll interpret Scripture to say it couldn't have happened. But I know it did. And I know something else. You don't ever want to feel what I felt or know what I know. You don't ever want to experience the lack of God's presence. I'm not talking about a lack of awareness that He is present, I'm talking about being fully aware that He is not.

I cried and I sobbed, but I knew it would not change the situation. I'd been offered a choice I couldn't make, a chance I couldn't take, and an opportunity to have what I was unable at that time to receive.

And so I slammed the doors of my glass prison shut once again and hoisted the pipe filled with poison to my lips as the fire once again melted the rocks into mind-numbing smoke.

The hazy grayish-white smoke filled the chamber and my lungs as I drew in deeply. And with the force of my exhale, the rush of the drug bombarded my brain and sent me into the stratosphere of a blistering high once again.

My skin felt flushed and hot, my pulse was racing and as my blood pressure skyrocketed with that familiar drenching of sweat through my pores, I looked down to where my heart was pounding so hard I could see it through my chest.

Nothing to Lose

Deciding to die because you have nothing to live for is easy. Deciding to live because you have nothing to lose takes a lot more thought. After all, deciding to die means you don't have to make any more decisions. Deciding to live means you have to make a lot more decisions and the first is deciding what to do next.

I hadn't thought that far ahead yet. But in deciding to live, it occurred to me that the Lord told me I had already died, and I figured if He wanted me to stay that way, He would not have come to have that talk with me in my room.

Besides, I had finished smoking all that cocaine which was enough to kill three people and it had taken so long to consume, that I passed out from exhaustion with one of the butane torches still burning in my hand. I woke up hours later still gripping that canister spewing fire and realized I should've burned up in my bed.

No, it seemed I had taken my best shot at dying and it just wasn't going to happen. And actually now that I think of it, I had accomplished dying, a few times. It was *staying* dead that wasn't working out.

That was the third time someone told me my heart had stopped and that I'd been dead before they brought me back. But this was the first time I could say I was truly grateful. I still had nothing to live for, but having nothing to lose can be very liberating.

After that encounter with God in my room, I knew that I could not live without Him. I hadn't yet figured out how to live *with* Him, but I knew I could not live without Him.

I had been scared plenty of times, but never that scared. I had never been that desperate and I had never been that alone. When I finally came down from that coke days later, the reality of God's absence set in again and I wept for days. I lay right there in my bed in the mess of my life, the mess of my room, and the messy remains of my week-long cocaine binge and cried like a baby.

> After that encounter with God, I knew that I could not live without Him.

I cried and I begged. I begged God to hear me. I begged God to save me. I begged God to come back. With all my might and with no other thought in my mind for days, I petitioned this

God whom I had finally met but still didn't know, to please come back because I knew I could not go on living without Him.

And then, as suddenly as He had come and then gone, He was back. Things were back to the way they had been. He wasn't talking to me and there was no particular manifestation of His presence, but He was no longer withholding Himself from me.

> My days of smoking thousands of dollars worth of cocaine at a time were gone.

It would have been just like all the years before when He had been present but I had ignored Him, except now that I had experienced the absence of His presence, I was aware that He was surrounding me again.

As far as knowing God, living for God, serving God, I still had no clue. And I was still very much a drug addict even though the loss of my paycheck had forced me into a kind of *economic rehab*. You don't have to be locked away in a rehab center if you just don't have any money.

I was still able to beg, borrow and steal a few bucks here and there, but my days of smoking thousands of dollars worth of cocaine at a time were gone. There was a lifestyle to lead where you could do that without a high-paying job, but I was still Frank Turner which meant going that far just wasn't an option.

What is Your Dream Job?

Have you ever thought about what you would do if you

had no mortgage to pay, no car note to make and no family to feed? What would you do if you had to start all over again from scratch and you could choose from just about anything, with the knowledge that technically you couldn't fail because you had nothing to lose?

What would you do if you were free to do anything?

What is the occupation, career or pursuit that would give you the most pleasure even if it didn't have a decent paycheck? What would you do if you were free to do anything? What is your dream job?

The fact is, before I was fired I was actually very disenchanted with the television news industry and often daydreamed about what my dream job would be.

The TV news business had been in a steady decline for nearly two decades and over the eight years before I got fired, there had been a particular downward spiral. There was a lot less substance to what we were reporting and a lot more "flash and trash." There was a growing and extremely heavy emphasis on *just getting people to watch* rather than concern about *what we were actually giving them to watch.*

Insiders used to joke that if people would sit and watch one of those old TV test patterns, interrupted by an occasional commercial, then that's all we'd put on the air. That's not much of an exaggeration. Trust me, viewers of today are getting a lot less than they used to, because television managers have discovered that you'll settle for it.

But before I got canned, I was seriously considering what else I might be able to do for a living. The problem was that I was trapped. I'd been doing so little for so long and getting paid so much, there was really no one else who would pay me as much for doing as little.

Anchoring a newscast is really easy if you have the aptitude, talent and love for it; and for the longest time, I found it to be really fun. Sometimes the hours were long, but mostly I did a little writing and a lot of talking. And for me, getting paid to talk is in itself a dream job.

In fact, I liked *what* I did all the way to the end. I just didn't particularly care for the *way* I had to do it, and of course my drug addiction had grown to the point where I was finding it increasingly hard to do it at all.

I hated more than anything that I had lost my job and my career and indeed my entire life, and more than *what I lost*, I hated *the way I lost it*.

Now that I was taking the "let's stick around, I've got nothing to lose, let's just see what happens" approach to life, the whole job decision thing was more than an idle question.

And make no mistake: my life was an *extreme mess*. It was actually beyond disaster.

I had publicly lost my career in a blaze of disgrace that meant also losing the job which represented my entire income and the pinnacle of everything I had worked more than twenty years to that point to achieve.

I was completely humiliated, my name and reputation

were destroyed, I was not only unemployed but unemployable. I was already filing for bankruptcy, my condo was in foreclosure, my car was being repossessed and all my credit cards, maxed out for cocaine, were cancelled.

I had no relatives to turn to and was too toxic to rely on friends, of which I really didn't have any with whom I could live or be temporarily supported.

I was still being sued with a ridiculous and trumped up fraud complaint over the credit card charges involving the phone sex for which the amounts had been extremely exaggerated and grossly misrepresented in the newspapers—newspapers that, by the way, all failed to report that the lawsuit was basically going to be dismissed until I was a no show in court. Even in the end after litigation, it was decided in my favor because it had no merit.

> Newspapers all failed to report that the lawsuit was decided in my favor because it had no merit.

I was lost, alone and lonely, I had nowhere to turn and no one to turn to. I was still completely addicted to the cocaine which I could no longer afford but still caused me to shake and tremble at the mere thought of it.

I was suffering severe depression and crippling panic and anxiety attacks for which I was afraid to have medication, because my constant bouts with the suicidal thoughts that emerged every time I laid out the reality of my situation like I'm doing now, made me want to take the entire bottle.

I had a cigarette habit I couldn't afford, a dog I couldn't feed and utilities that I was juggling minimum payments on just trying not to end up in the dark or cut off without a phone.

And to top it all off, I was kind of becoming afraid to leave the house because I couldn't even go to the grocery store without people staring, pointing and whispering. Even in my building, a trip to the mailbox or out to walk the dog meant an excruciating pass

> I couldn't go to the grocery store without people staring.

through the lobby which I always tried to hurry through before any one could ask me a question.

It was beyond humiliation, it was beyond disaster, and the whole mess seemed far beyond repair. My life was a mess and I had made a colossal mess of everything in it.

But on the bright side: *that meant I had nothing to lose.*

CHAPTER SEVEN

ONLY THE TRUTH IS FUNNY

A merry heart does good, *like* medicine,
But a broken spirit dries the bones
(Proverbs 17:22).

S tandup comedy. Yep, that's what I chose. I looked at the full spectrum of promising choices, potential fallbacks, possible career moves and after careful consideration, decided to put all my eggs in a basket labeled "Standup Comedy."

I hadn't even told a joke, but just the idea had people laughing already.

"So you think you're funny huh?" That was the standard question. "Well tell me a joke!" That was the standard follow-up demand.

What the person actually meant was "You're crazy, but you're not funny and I'll prove it to you. Tell me one of the lame jokes you plan to do in your 'act' and I'll just stand here and stare at you like the audience would and save you the trouble and embarrassment of actually having to get on stage."

People can be so encouraging.

I didn't know it at the time, but God actually did have a

wonderful plan for me and a big part of it included this ridiculous foray into the world of standup comedy. It was not going to be my new career, but it was going to be very useful.

> God actually did have a wonderful plan for me, and it included standup comedy.

And it really didn't turn out to be all that ridiculous. First of all, I *am* funny. I've always had a wonderful sense of humor and my quick wit was among the elements which made me a very entertaining and successful news anchor.

Second, doing standup is basically getting someone to pay you for talking, which was, after all, my specialty.

Third, when I finally got a shot at "Open Mike Night" at Mark Ridley's Comedy Castle in Royal Oak, Michigan; I *killed. I absolutely killed.* (That means I did well in comedy lingo.)

When I delayed my entrance on stage for a few seconds after my name was announced and then emerged with the line, "Sorry I'm late, I got hung up on the phone." the audience roared.

I did fifteen minutes of solid material and rocked the house. My jokes were peppered with profanity and included a lot of vulgar themes that I'm uncomfortable with now, but at the time I was very proud and a lot of people thought I had promise. I got a great review in the next day's newspaper.

People were still laughing over the idea of me being a comedian. But this time they were laughing with me.

Finally and most importantly, doing a brief stint of standup gave me two of the most important features of my life: it took me from in front of the cameras where I had always been the most comfortable and put me in front of a live audience so I could learn how to handle a crowd, which was God preparing me to be a preacher, and it brought me together with the woman for whom my entire life was being designed, my wife Nicky. That was God finally preparing me to be a husband.

Between my name recognition and the positive reviews, suddenly I was getting booked in comedy clubs all over the Metro Detroit area. The pay was terrible, sometimes as little as fifty bucks a set, which was not bad for seven to fifteen minutes of work, but it wasn't going to make a living.

I was also picking up some very steady part-time work as a fill-in host of a call-in program on a local talk-radio station. Aside from the extra income, which I desperately needed to even hope to be able to smoke a little cocaine occasionally, that also gave me an outlet to advertise some of my bookings.

Doing comedy was tons of fun and got me out of the house and it was extremely therapeutic. It provided an avenue for me

No matter how sad the facts may be; only the truth is funny.

to emerge back into the public eye while shedding some of the embarrassment of my recent past by turning it into material for comedy.

All the ugly stuff I couldn't shake from my life, the

stuff about which I was continually depressed and occasionally contemplating suicide, I added to my act. It was cathartic and quite entertaining. Indeed I found out that in comedy no matter how sad the facts may be, only the truth is funny.

Wow! What a Woman

Of the few people I initially told I had an interest in trying to do standup there was one who didn't laugh, but instead picked up the phone and called a friend of hers who was a successful comedienne.

> I went to the home of Alyce Faye and changed the course of my life.

A few days later, I went to the home of Alyce Faye and changed the course of my life. She had closely followed my news career and told me that I had always been her favorite television personality. She was as excited to meet me as I was to meet her.

We became instant friends and because she was very maternal, it was like having a new mother in my life, a real authentic nurturing mother. God had just put something in Alyce's heart that made her love me.

I told her I had always secretly wanted to be a comedian and had actually planned a career as an actor and entertainer before I accidentally got sidetracked by a life in radio and television broadcasting and journalism.

She told me about her life on the stage, about doing

comedy and performing, about the ups and downs, the traveling, the cutthroat nightclub owners and the backstabbing comedians who stole material and tried to sabotage other comics' gigs.

It was obvious that she loved every minute of it and she made it sound even more enticing to me and was so encouraging, I shed any doubt that I really could be successful.

She asked me about everything going on in my life and I was able to talk freely with her about my trials and tribulations without fear of judgment.

She was a lot like the memories I had created of my mother. She was beautiful, warm and extremely heavy. Her weight was causing problems with her health and she was always struggling with one diet or another.

When Alyce died less than eighteen months later from lung cancer that had spread to her brain, it was likely that her obesity had contributed to the cancer's rapid spread. I was crushed by her death, but because of her, I had a whole new life waiting in my future that had nothing to do with why I thought we had been brought together.

It was Alyce who worked with me initially and dedicated herself to teaching me the business of doing comedy: booking gigs, writing material, and learning about timing. It was with her that I learned that in comedy, only the truth is funny and that timing *is* everything.

But the greatest thing that Alyce did for me was set me up on the blind date with her niece that opened my eyes to love for the rest of my life.

I met Nicky Simmons on Wednesday June 17, 1998 at 7:20 in the evening. I was twenty minutes late because I couldn't make up my mind about going to Alyce's house to meet her. It was just supposed to be a casual meeting for a meaningless date with no strings attached, but it still made me nervous.

It was love at first sight.

I had been through so much, was still quite unstable, and the last thing I needed to attempt was even a casual relationship.

Frank Turner, Mark Ridley and Alyce Faye at Frank's Comedy Castle Debut, 1998.

But Alyce had spoken so highly of how extremely intelligent and beautiful her niece was that I was intrigued enough to go, even if not courageous enough to be on time.

When I walked into Alyce's home and into her living room I saw Nicky and nearly passed out. All I could think was *Wow! What a woman!*

I'd forgotten to take off the pair of sunglasses I routinely hid behind to avoid eye contact with strangers and so Nicky thought I was being a little "too cool" for her tastes. But as soon as I realized I had them on, I pulled them away from my face and looked her in the eyes.

It's the craziest thing, but it was love at first sight. I didn't know how, but I knew she was going to be the next Mrs. Turner and the only one to never be an *ex*-Mrs. Turner.

We went on our date, to the comedy club, in fact. We laughed and talked on the way and were holding hands by the time we got there. We've been by each other's side ever since.

That night, the God I had just recently met, but still didn't know reached down from Heaven to place into my life a little deposit from the infinite riches He was

> Nicky can be as comfortable around the homeless as she is in the finest homes of splendor.

prepared to bestow. He gave me the heart of my wife and the love of my life.

It was clear from the first moment I met her that Nicky is a singularly special woman—kind and gentle, yet determined and strong willed, she is very sensitive, creative and loving. Nicky can be as comfortable around the homeless as she is in the finest homes of splendor. She is the perfect mother, the greatest companion, the best friend and the most exciting wife.

The day I met Nicky was the day that I made up my mind that no matter what, the old Frank Turner would somehow have to die, so that a new Frank Turner, fit to be with this woman could spend the rest of his life making her dreams come true.

She made me feel that way from the moment I laid eyes on her that Wednesday, June 17, 1998 at 7:20, and she has continued

Frank and Nicky on a date.

to make me strengthen that resolve every day since. *Wow! What a woman!*

Isn't Love Grand?

Falling in love with Nicky was the most wonderful thing that could've happened to me right from the moment I met her. For her, though, falling in love with me was...well...not so much.

She was a divorced mother of two young teenagers with a full-time job, a full-time life and full-time responsibilities. She had an insurance career she was trying to advance, college classes she was trying to complete and bills she was trying to pay off.

Even though she wasn't looking, it was the perfect time

> It was the *absolute worst time* to meet someone like... well...*like me.*

in her life to meet someone special, responsible, selfless and committed, but it was the *absolute worst time* to meet someone like...well...*like me.*

She had no idea that I was such an emotional cripple or that I still had a raging drug addiction, bouts of severe depression, panic attacks and a general demeanor of confusion about my past, present *and* future.

She had no idea that not only was I unable to provide any help to her, but that soon I would begin to siphon off her resources to feed my drug addiction and begin to drag her down with me.

Like I said before, I knew that I would have to kill off the old Frank Turner in order to be fit for Nicky, but the slow death I was dying wasn't nearly fast enough to keep her out of my harm's way.

Because she lived seventy miles from the Detroit area in Lansing, and didn't own a TV that was hooked up to anything but a VCR, Nicky had never even heard of me. She didn't have a clue concerning what I had been through with the exception of tidbits she'd been told by Alyce.

I'm sure Alyce sugar coated what she knew, and honestly, even Alyce only knew what she had read in the paper. I had told her a lot about my emotions, but virtually nothing about the drugs.

By the time our relationship had grown close enough and deep enough and intimate enough for her to see all the cracks, potholes, chips, dings, wounds and scars of my addictions and dementia, Nicky was beginning to have serious second thoughts and realized that investing in me as her future didn't look like a wise choice.

I would have advised her to "run away from Frank Turner screaming as if he were on fire" had I been speaking as an impartial friend. But as the man for whom she had become like the air I breathed, I tried everything I could to make sure that as bad as I was, I always stayed just good enough to keep her from ditching me.

I didn't make it.

But there was something about that apartment of mine being a meeting place for God. And I wasn't the only one there with whom God decided to visit and have a little chat.

Long before I had even dreamed of sharing with Nicky the experience I had with God talking to me in the midst of a cocaine overdose in my bedroom, she came to me one day, tears in her eyes, to tell me that she had heard the voice of God in the guest bathroom shower!

"Stay with him," she told me He said. "He needs you."

> "Stay with him," the Lord told her. "He needs you."

Unbeknownst to me, the voice of God Nicky heard in the shower was a direct contradiction to the voice she was hearing in

Frank and Nicky. Wow! What a woman!

her head. Just as the voice of her thoughts was deciding how to break the news to me that she needed to get on with her life, the voice of God overruled that plan and told her to stay.

Only the truth is funny.

Nicky didn't know God any more than I did. She had spent a lot of her life in churches; I hadn't been since I was a kid. Both of us had been religious at times in our lives, but neither had actually met the Lord or been born again and saved by the blood of His Son. In fact, if you had asked either of us at the time what

Frank and Nicky. Isn't love grand?

that even meant, we couldn't have explained it to you if we had the whole Bible to use as a cheat sheet.

What are the chances of these two people at separate times, neither with a relationship with God, just imagining they're hearing the voice of the manifest presence of God, in the same apartment, especially without her knowing anything of my previous experience?

None! The probability of that happening is zero! This was no hallucinogenic coincidence. This was simply God meeting two people He intended to be together by speaking to them in the one place most likely to tear them apart.

I'm convinced there was a demonic presence in that apartment that had been out to destroy me from the moment I moved in. There had been some wonderful and happy times over the years I lived in that apartment, but they had been far outweighed and overshadowed by drug use, depression, anxiety and dysfunction.

I'd met with the devil himself over crack cocaine many times in that apartment. I fatally overdosed twice in that apartment, once ending up in the emergency room at Beaumont Hospital in Royal Oak.

I'd wallowed in some of the most disgusting pornography and indulged some of the most demented thoughts in that apartment. I had one of the most severe panic attacks in that apartment, so intense that my eyes were actually shooting projectile tears from the force of my crying.

And now it was that very same apartment and the way it

made me feel that was threatening to destroy the new life I had a chance to make with Nicky.

It was the hold that apartment had on me and the things I was always doing there that had convinced her to cut her losses and cut me loose.

Whenever she came to visit me there, she was always afraid of what she would find. Even though she didn't condone any of my drug use, the smell of marijuana being smoked when she used her key to open my door was at least an indication that the last batch of cocaine hadn't killed me.

It was in that apartment that I tried to convince her to smoke cocaine with me, but thank God she adamantly refused. It was to that apartment I would always run, often in the middle of the night from her place in Lansing, because I couldn't ignore the call of the pipe long enough to enjoy a few days away.

And it was in that apartment that she would always find me when I would be AWOL for days, and finally in frustration, she would come looking for me.

There was a lot of emotional sickness in me, but that apartment had a demonic sickness in it and it seems the only way for God to make Himself and His presence and His plans known was to show up there in His glory and use His voice to get someone's attention directly.

"Stay with him," the voice of the Lord told her. "He needs you."

And the first thing I needed her to do was help get me out of that apartment for good.

The Great Escape

I needed to escape that apartment *for* Nicky, but I also could not have escaped it *without* her. An eviction date had been set as a result of the foreclosure. I had to be out before then, even though we were both anxious to get me out of there as soon as possible.

The problem was that before cocaine had sucked all the money out of my life, I acquired a lot of stuff: furniture, clothing, appliances, dishes——it all had to go and we couldn't afford to pay someone to move it. We had to do it ourselves and we needed a truck.

All of my credit card accounts were closed in the bankruptcy and the U-Haul rental wouldn't take cash as a deposit, not that I had enough cash anyway.

Nicky had to use her credit card for the deposit as well as pay for the truck before she came up to the apartment with me to help pack everything and then help lug it all down in the elevator from the twenty-third floor of my building.

Thank God she was able to do what God said and not what I would've done, because in spite of the voice of God, I would have left me right there.

We got a couple of hand trucks and went to work loading a moving truck nearly the size of a semi and packed it solid from front to back.

Sofas, love seats, chairs and tables; a refrigerator, washer and dryer; a complete living room, dining room, bedroom and a sleeper sofa; she packed at least eight wardrobes of clothes and countless boxes of miscellaneous stuff and then helped me haul it all down to the truck and pack it inside.

We've often talked since about how God must've shown up again.

He didn't say anything that time, but He had to have done a lot of the work. It took us the entire day and into the wee hours of the next to get everything out of that apartment, and even as hard and fast and efficiently as we worked; sweating, toiling and completely wearing ourselves out; there is still no way for two mere mortal human beings to have accomplished what we did. It was a supernatural feat.

It was early the next morning by the time we were done and had driven that truck to Lansing. Nicky had to be up to get ready for a new day at work before she could even put the old day to bed.

Our hands were cut, scraped and bleeding; our muscles ached from head to toe, and our feet were so sore that we could hardly walk. And that's when we remembered that the truck had to be emptied and returned to the rental office back in Southfield before the twenty-four hour deadline or we (meaning Nicky) would be charged for another day that we (meaning Nicky) couldn't afford.

Only the truth is funny. Now.

(Are you starting to understand why I have dedicated my life to the care, comfort and concerns of this woman?)

The good news was that even if she wanted to slap me,

we were so sore and in such bad shape that Nicky couldn't have possibly lifted her hand high enough to hit me.

The bad news was that there was no way we were going to be able to unload the furniture and large appliances by ourselves. It was also then that we realized it wasn't all going to fit in her condo anyway. So we ended up calling a used furniture and appliance store. They sent over a truck, bought most of the heavy stuff and unloaded it from our truck to theirs. We dragged the rest into Nicky's basement and garage.

The store paid me just about enough to cover the cost of the truck, which meant I had talked Nicky into helping me move all that stuff to Lansing for the privilege of ending up with just a bit less money than if we had left it all back in the apartment. What a goof! Praise God that I've grown a lot since then.

But you know, in spite of how stupid that was, not once has she ever thrown that incident up in my face. Not once has she ever mentioned it at all except to say how much she admired me for working so hard that day and packing the truck so skillfully.

Wow! What a woman.

CHAPTER EIGHT

RAISED FROM THE DEAD

Jesus said to her, "I am the resurrection and the life.
He who believes in Me, though he may die, he shall
live. And whoever lives and believes in Me
shall never die. Do you believe this?"
(John 11:25–26).

When you roll the stone away from the tomb of what my life had become by the day the Lord Jesus Christ called me from death into eternal salvation, you get an odor reminiscent of what must've wafted from the tomb of Lazarus after he had been decomposing for four days.

My relationship with Nicky had grown and improved, but largely because of her commitment to obey the voice of God rather than from great strides of my progress. I was showing only minimal signs of improvement.

In the two months since moving in with her, I'd only slipped away once to smoke cocaine. But I had still been hitting the weed pretty hard and I was drinking a lot. I was eating her out of house and home, mostly to stave off depression, and I had gained about eighty pounds since we met.

I was still struggling with the addiction, fighting a losing battle with depression, and even though I was working steadily at the radio station, I was being more irresponsible with the money than I was helping with her budget.

And yet somehow, by the grace of God, I was managing to love her. All that I had once used for the manipulation of women, I was now able to genuinely give to her.

She had longed to be known, heard, learned, regarded, valued and cherished. And so as best I could, I studied her, listened to her, absorbed her and gazed into her, treasured and appreciated her.

> Neither of us regards the concept of race, the consideration of status, or the worship of wealth.

We openly shared every facet of ourselves and found that we had a remarkable list of things in common for a black man from the south side of Chicago and a white woman from Howell, in Livingston County which was once the headquarters of the Ku Klux Klan in Michigan.

Neither of us regards the concept of race, the consideration of status, or the worship of wealth. We both love art, music and education and hate tension, ignorance and bad manners.

She is, to this day, the only person I know besides me who can sing every note and every word to every song on Elton John's *Goodbye Yellow Brick Road* double album.

We both love deep discussion but hate divisive debate. We can be captivated by the simplest of things like flowers, trees and chipmunks; appreciative of treasured things like gold, silver and precious stones; and satisfied by valuable things like honesty, character, diligence and integrity. We like our promises to be priceless and hate when those of others aren't. And if we give our word, you've gotten the most valuable thing we have.

Rarely had anyone sought or valued her opinion and I cherished her wisdom. She had always lacked encouragement and I have always exhorted her to recognize how awesome she is at everything she sets her mind to accomplish.

In many ways, my incapacitation was a burden that she was growing weary of carrying

Our relationship was becoming of such emotional value to her that she couldn't walk away.

and yet our relationship was becoming of such emotional value to her that she couldn't walk away.

From the day we were both conceived, Nicky and I had a date with destiny and everything that had happened to this point was leading us to it.

After we got married we looked back at many of the cards, notes and letters we exchanged while we were dating. We were surprised to see that in many, if not most of them, there was the mention of God concerning our future. We often wrote to each other that we thought we were "blessed" to be together.

We often expressed that we felt "God" had arranged our meeting and had a plan for our lives. It's remarkable because as I said, we had both dabbled in religion, Nicky had even regularly attended church for much of her life, but neither of us actually had a relationship with nor even knew the one true and living God personally.

Aside from those references we would have these long

conversations by cell phone as I drove back and forth from the radio job in Southfield. I would tell her about specific revelations I was having and she would recognize passages of Scripture in what I related was suddenly on my mind. I had never been a Bible reader and couldn't quote Scripture to save my life; at least as far as I knew.

But sure enough, I'd get home and she'd get out her Bible and she would find the specific passages I had been quoting direct revelation from. It was scary and yet very exciting. I wanted to tell her about the Lord speaking to me in the apartment, but I just figured she'd think I'd been hallucinating from the drugs.

But the time had finally come for more to change about me than I could ever make happen on my own. The time had come for the old me to die and the new Frank Turner to be raised from the dead.

Jesus Is Always Right On Time

Now Jesus loved Martha and her sister and Lazarus. So, when He heard that he was sick, He stayed two more days in the place where He was. Then after this He said to the disciples, "Let us go to Judea again" (John 11:5–7).

Though the pleas were urgent for him to come to Lazarus's side, *Jesus waited*. Because he loved Lazarus, Mary and Martha, *Jesus waited*. He could not be hindered but He also could not be hurried. *Jesus waited* because He *chose* to wait. And when it was time to go He told his disciples, "Let us go..."

It was time to go because Jesus had an appointment. He had an appointment with a grieving family; He had an appointment with an unbelieving crowd; He had an appointment with a man in a tomb. All of them needed to come together at the same time. It had to be the right time. It had to be the perfect time.

That Lazarus would meet death on the day Jesus was summoned was a collision course set before time began. There are no surprises in the eternal plan of God.

> You saw me before I was born. Every day of my life was recorded in your book. Every moment was laid out before a single day had passed (Psalm 139:16, NLT).

But the apparent end of his life was obviously only the beginning of Lazarus' real story. And the time between Lazarus being placed in the tomb dead and emerging alive was time orchestrated by Jesus. And again, it comes back to our good and God's glory.

> So when Jesus came, He found that he had already been in the tomb four days (John 11:17).

> Jesus said, "Take away the stone." Martha, the sister of him who was dead, said to Him, "Lord,

by this time there is a stench, for he has been *dead* four days" (John 11:39).

By raising Lazarus only after he had been buried and was beginning to decompose, the Lord Jesus gave us, and those who witnessed him being raised first hand, a rock solid foundation for faith. That is for *our good.* And by assuring that no one, absolutely no one, but God could be credited with restoring Lazarus from his decomposed state, *God gets the glory.*

If you're in a desperate situation right now or know someone who is and you're wondering why the Lord isn't yet there at your side, give Him time and consider His plan for Lazarus.

Jesus received a desperate plea to come right away. But He knew that it would be more for our good and give God more glory for Him to wait until the perfect time.

As my daily drug use had rendered me incapable of performing my duties at work, *Jesus waited.* As I was suspended and my firing was imminent, *Jesus waited.* As I was fired, publicly disgraced, humiliated and contemplated suicide, *Jesus waited.*

> Like Lazarus, the apparent end of my life was only the beginning of my real story.

Because He loved me as well as all the people whose faith would be ignited and strengthened by the result of their prayers for me, *Jesus waited.*

Like Lazarus, the apparent end of my life was only the

beginning of my real story. The time between *losing* my career, my relationships, my reputation and everything I had, even my life; and *gaining* all I now have in Christ was time orchestrated by Jesus.

Maximizing the Moment

The Lord Jesus Christ knows exactly the moment when His work will have the greatest effect; that moment is usually after it is clearly too late for anyone or anything else to help.

In the time that Jesus waited, all hope for Lazarus was lost. His family had watched him die. They had a funeral and buried him in his tomb. Family members and friends began to look ahead to how they would go on in a world without him.

> Millions of people had watched me "die."

After I was fired in 1998, all hope for me was lost as well. There was no hope for the restoration of my career, there was no hope for my rehabilitation from drug and alcohol addiction, and there was no hope for deliverance from my demons of depression and anxiety.

A viewing public made up of millions of people had watched me "die." They had a funeral for me in their minds and I buried myself in the "tomb" of my condo. With the doors locked and the shades drawn, I was "buried" within the confines of my high-rise condominium "tomb."

In the same way Jesus waited as the stench of death began

to fill Lazarus' tomb, He waited as the stench of my destroyed life filled my condo.

And by waiting, Jesus assures that He not only will maximize the impact on those who will be assembled for His arrival, but especially on the person whose miraculous rescue He is coming to perform.

As for the visit to Bethany, Jesus' disciples were concerned because the Lord faced opposition and threats there. When the time was right for His return, He was able to assure His disciples that their safety was guaranteed in the fact that He had a purpose to fulfill. That's a good lesson for Christians.

When we are walking in the purpose Jesus has determined for our lives, we need not fear any opposition or threat. When we are going *where* He would have us go, *when* He would have us go and for the *purpose* He has ordained, we can go forward boldly and confidently in His name.

But that doesn't mean we'll always understand right away *why* we are following the Lord on a particular journey.

> These things He said, and after that He said to them,
> "Our friend Lazarus sleeps, but I go that I may wake
> him up." Then His disciples said, "Lord, if he sleeps
> he will get well." However, Jesus spoke of his death,
> but they thought that He was speaking about taking
> rest in sleep (John 11:11–13).

The mission of Jesus was a mystery to His disciples. Jesus knew His friend was dead and his body rotting. His disciples thought Lazarus was resting and getting better.

To Jesus, it was a matter of waiting for the worst and then making it better, while His disciples thought it might be best to just leave well enough alone.

While Jesus was planning the miracle of bringing forth life out of death, His disciples assumed He was merely going to ruin a good nap and disturb Lazarus from a sound sleep.

> Jesus was planning the miracle of bringing forth life out of death.

Obviously they didn't get it. Today's followers of Jesus are often just as likely to miss the point.

As we follow the Lord, we are often afraid because we don't fully understand the security and safety we have in trusting Him.

As we follow the Lord, we don't always immediately understand why we must go in a certain direction at a particular time.

As we follow the Lord, we may not realize the depth of the problem waiting to be solved ahead or the height of glory it will bring to God. And there are times when we might think all someone needs is to be left alone, when in fact what they really need is to be touched by Jesus.

But faith in Christ is not a blind faith. He doesn't require or desire us to follow Him in ignorance, only in faith. Faith in

Christ does not require you to be led without knowing where you are being taken, but it does require trusting Him to take you where you need to be.

> Faith in Christ is to know that He is always the answer and without Him all hope is lost.

Faith in Christ doesn't require you to be ignorant of *your purpose*, but you must be willing to trust in *His plan*. Faith in Christ is to know that He is always the answer and without Him, all hope is lost.

But perhaps the most important element of faith in Christ is being ready to receive the blessing that can only be found in the last place you'd look.

> Then Jesus said to them plainly, "Lazarus is dead. And I am glad for your sakes that I was not there, that you may believe. Nevertheless let us go to him" (John 11:14–15).

Now we find the Lord speaking to His disciples in plain terms so that no further misunderstanding is possible. He has reached the point with them where they must be aware of the gravity of the situation so that they can be blessed by the miracle that lies ahead.

Lazarus, He tells them, is dead. With that they know much more about the character of their mission. They are going to help someone who is otherwise beyond help. They are traveling with the man who is *the* hope where no other hope exists.

And yet, while they now know the destination is Bethany and they know the *purpose* is to help Lazarus, they still don't know the *plan*.

How was Lazarus helped by being allowed to die? Why is Jesus glad that He wasn't there to help him? How could it possibly be good for the disciples' sakes that Jesus was not there when Lazarus seemingly needed Him the most?

They know the *purpose* is to go and see about Lazarus, but they don't know the *plan* is to change the hearts of untold numbers of people by what Jesus will do when He gets there.

Just before Jesus responded to the prayers and petitions on my behalf, it became very clear that I, too, was essentially dead.

Unknown to the public, I had already suffered my third fatal cocaine overdose since taking and losing the evening anchor chair. Addiction had become the controlling factor of my life.

My reputation had been damaged beyond repair and my

> Suicide became my obsession. Daily, I was consumed with taking my life.

career in television, to which I had devoted the majority of my life, was over. Suicide became my obsession. Daily, I was consumed with taking my life. Each day I dreamed of the sweet relief that I believed could only be found in the grave.

What neither I nor anyone around me knew was that I was being blessed by every moment the Lord Jesus delayed in coming to my rescue. Only by allowing my condition to deteriorate beyond all help and beyond all hope, would people understand the gravity of the situation and be blessed by the miracle that was to come.

The *purpose* of God for my life was always that I would be rescued by Jesus and that thousands of others would be involved through their agreement in prayer for me. But the *plan* of God involved rescuing me in the way that would have the deepest impact on the greatest number of people.

> "And I am glad for your sakes that I was not there, that you may believe. Nevertheless let us go to him" (John 11:15).

But finally there was that moment when the present time became the right time. This was the moment when the *promise* of God and *purpose* of God would come together to change the *people* of God.

Jesus was coming. Lazarus was soon to be raised from the dead. An overwhelming miracle was about to catapult a crowd into salvation through faith in Christ. The crowd that was soon to be assembled would be focused on Lazarus' tomb breathlessly waiting to see if he would really be able to answer the call of Jesus.

The moment was coming when all that had plagued Lazarus, all that had claimed his life, and all that had seemed to seal his fate and seal him in his grave was about to change for our good and God's glory.

But first there would have to be a disturbing revelation.

The stone at the entrance to Lazarus' tomb would have to be rolled away. The stench from deep inside his grave would have to be exposed.

It was the main reason Jesus waited. By waiting for the smell of death to be unmistakable, it would have the greatest impact on every witness. The indescribable smell of death would leave an impression that, combined with the shock of seeing Lazarus called back to life by Jesus, would convince people that He was the Messiah.

There was a parallel moment in my life. It was August 15, 1999. It was the moment that divided my life into "before" and "after." It was a moment that permanently changed me and would have the power to change all who know me and would come to know my testimony.

Jesus had come. Frank Turner was soon to be raised from the dead. I was standing in the baptismal pool at Greater Apostolic Faith Church in Detroit. There was a crowd assembled. The baptistry had the full attention of the packed church as one of the most joyful and exciting parts of the Sunday worship service was happening.

In this moment, new believers in Christ were being baptized. We would be immersed in Christ's blood, washed in the water of His Word, baptized into His death and burial then pulled out of the water and into His resurrection to walk in the newness of life.

The Bible calls it the outward manifestation of an inward good conscience toward God. It was quite a moment.

And in that moment, many who had prayed for me were breathlessly waiting to see what would happen when I answered the call of Jesus.

But in opening my "tomb" to free me from the grave of addiction and call me to life from death in my trespasses and sins, the fullness of the stench from my tomb would also have to be released.

> Many who had prayed for me were breathlessly waiting to see what would happen.

And like the stench emanating from Lazarus' tomb, the evidence would make it clear to every observer that I had truly been dead and that the act of raising and restoring me was truly a miracle.

Hearing is Believing

So then faith *comes* by hearing, and hearing by the word of God (Romans 10:17).

If on any given day before we were born again, you had asked Nicky or me if Jesus was the Son of God we most certainly would have said yes, even though neither of us had a clue what that meant. For our entire lives we had accepted the premise that Jesus is the Lord who was crucified for the sin of the world; that He has risen from the grave and ascended to Heaven and even that His return to judge the living and the dead is imminent.

We've always believed all of that, but never had a clue what any of it was supposed to actually mean to us, and never saw any value or *power* that believing it could bring to our lives or to anyone we knew. That was all about to change.

But the change would require that God show us His true power because previously, all I'd

> *Religion* is where divine truth meets human opinion.

known concerning the things of God were empty, vain, powerless and *religious*. I'd recognized early in life that religion is the breeding ground of hypocrisy. I've always hated it and I was thrilled to learn that God hates religion more than I and has held it in contempt for far longer.

Saying that *God hates religion* is a strong statement that is hard for some to bear. But the Bible confirms that, so we better be clear about what we're actually saying.

Religion is where the truth of God is tainted by the doctrine of man; it's where divine truth meets human opinion; it is where the false gods and practices of mankind's imagination are given equal footing with the one true and living God of the Bible.

Religion is any *system* whereby people try to establish *their own* righteousness by *following that system*, rather than by submitting themselves to the righteousness of God.

The righteousness of God, in no uncertain terms, is the Lord Jesus Christ Himself. True Christianity, therefore, is not a religion meant to be practiced by following a system; it is a relationship to be lived in the love of God obtained by faith in

His Son.

True Christianity is actually the born again person's relationship with Christ; it is the only true and living relationship with the only true and living God through the person of His Son and our Savior, the Lord Jesus Christ.

The Bible tells us that whoever *has the Son* has eternal life:

> He who has the Son has life; he who does not have
> the Son of God does not have life (1 John 5:12).

Notice that the Scripture speaks nothing of a rule, nothing of a ritual, nothing of a tradition that can bring eternal life. There is only a true relationship of faith in the Son and that can only happen by being born again by the Spirit of God.

> **True Christianity is actually the born again person's relationship with Christ.**

Sometimes well meaning, Bible believing, born again Christians who are either uninformed or careless with their terms refer to their *true Christianity* as a *religion*. This certainly adds to the confusion *because Christianity that is **not real** can actually **still be practiced as a religion.***

Let me give you an analogy. You can belong to a fan club without ever having a relationship with, or even meeting, the person around whom the fan club revolves.

By the same token, there are many people who belong to a

church or a denomination in a capacity that amounts to little more than membership in Christ's fan club, but they have never actually met or formed a living personal relationship with Him for their salvation.

> You can be a member of a church and never know the Lord Jesus Christ personally.

You can be a charter member of a fan club in good standing and never know the object of the club's affection personally. And you can be a charter member of a church in good standing and never know the person of our salvation, the Lord Jesus Christ, personally.

I have preached the gospel to church members, people who had sat on the pew for years, even pastors, who finally got saved because, for the first time, they actually truly crossed over the line from *empty false religion*. They entered the living saving relationship with the Lord Jesus Christ and were born again.

> Jesus answered and said to him, "Most assuredly, I say to you, unless one is born again, he cannot see the kingdom of God" (John 3:3).

> Everyone who believes that Jesus is the Christ is born of God, and everyone who loves the father loves his child as well (1 John 5:1, NIV).

Because I hated religion even before I was saved, I never

cared much for preachers, pastors, priests, ministers, reverends or rabbis. And as far as I was concerned, empty religion was all anybody was preaching and the only people preaching that were religious hypocrites.

That, of course, isn't true. There is a world of people preaching the true gospel of salvation in Christ, but after years of suffering from disappointment and disillusionment and intimate experience with false religion, it was what I had come to believe. And that was what the Lord had to break through in order for me to hear the truth and be saved.

But years of precedent cemented into my background were still standing in the way of that. My religious experience began before my mother died; in the Catholic school she enrolled me in as a kindergartner, where we began to learn the Roman Catholic system of catechism as a required element of our parochial education.

My grandmother, who only hung out at Baptist and African Methodist Episcopal Churches, and not even those regularly, made me continue to go to Catholic Church every Sunday after my mother died, but she refused to go with me.

I actually only went when she gave me a check for the offering. If she gave me cash, I used it for lunch at the Museum of Science and Industry. If she gave me a check, I'd go to the Museum anyway, but I'd stop at the church on the way and drop the envelope in the offering box.

Even as a child, I could see that the ritualistic practices of Catholicism were empty of God as were the lives of the people I saw trapped into performing them.

And as I grew, so did my questions; but no one could give me straight answers to them:

- Why were we supposed to bow and genuflect in front of statues made of stone?

- How could lighting candles have any effect on people in some purgatory?

- Was purgatory really a place where its captives' freedom could be purchased by coins in a "poor box?" And had anyone *really* been sentenced there for not saying a rosary or for eating a hamburger on a Friday?

- What's the benefit of coming to a mass in Latin (as they were when I was a kid) of which I can't even understand a word?

- And if we believe the Bible, how come we never actually open one and study it?

All I ever got in response were more rules to obey, more rituals to perform and more traditions to uphold. Everybody was good at parroting the Catholic doctrine that was passed down from priests, but no one could offer any *insight or understanding* or the fire of the Holy Spirit that you could feel.

And nobody I knew, no matter how Catholic they were, was any different from anybody else.

Everybody acted like they were scared of God when they were in the church building, but I think it was actually the building that frightened them. If they were really scared of God, you would never imagine by their behavior that the same God who lived inside the church was the one who lived outside as well.

When they weren't in church (or for some, even when they were) all the Catholics I knew smoked and drank and cursed and had sex any way they wanted with whomever they pleased, and it seemed the only requirement was to carry the burden of feeling guilty about it and to spend a few moments a week with a priest in a wooden box for confession; and even then, only telling him half the story.

A Distinction without a Difference

The churches my grandmother liked were flashy, flamboyant, loud and just as worthless *in their empty practices*. I don't think very many of the people in her circle were born again, but they sure put on a good show. The choirs were big and loud, and by the time they were done they had the whole house revved up and ready for some preaching that was also big and loud.

The ladies in these places were funny. As a tradition, these churches usually had female attendants dressed in white uniforms who were called "Nurses." They always knew exactly who they were supposed to attend to.

It was the same couple of ladies all the time. They always wore fancy church dresses with lots of sequins and gigantic hats. As the choir would reach a crescendo, these gals would get very excited and start to jump up and down (as best they could for their age and girth). Then before long, they'd start hollering and shouting, and after checking to make sure someone was ready to catch them, they'd *suddenly* "get the vapors" or whatever, and appear to faint!

Sometimes they'd let out a low throaty, "Waaaaaaaaah" before throwing their arms in the air and "fainting." They'd lay there in the pew or the aisle while somebody, usually one of the nurses, fanned them.

Everybody knew they were faking and sometimes people who'd seen this act too many times would roll their eyes.

One time this lady, one of the regulars, was ready to "faint" and she thought the guy standing in the row behind her was someone who would catch her. He was not.

She let out a "Waaaaaaaaaaaaaaaah" and stretched her arms out to the side and fell straight back toward the man. Instead of stepping forward to grab her in his arms, he just stood there and watched her fall and hit her head on the back of the pew.

"Bonk!"

It was like somebody had bounced a coconut off the wood of that bench. That sister was knocked out for real and the Holy Ghost had nothing to do with it.

People were fanning her and splashing water in her face

as she started to come around. I laughed so hard I thought I was going to swallow my tongue. My grandmother looked at me and just grinned.

Later in the car on the way home, we talked about it again and again and laughed together all the way. When we got home, Grandmother got on the "hotline" with her other church friends. They talked and laughed and gossiped about that lady and everybody else they'd seen at church—whose dress was "tacky," whose hat was "too big," and whose wig "wasn't on straight." With each new call, she'd include the previous lady on her list of people to trash. I figured they were all doing the same concerning her too.

I always thought it would have been *really* funny if she'd accidentally called the wrong person and started trashing them to their face thinking she was talking to someone else.

Caught in the Act

On the first Sunday of the month, Grandmother liked to get to church early and stay all day. We would have breakfast, then Sunday school, followed by the morning service; then lunch, the Missionary ladies meeting in the afternoon (I don't know why they called these ladies Missionaries, they never went anywhere or did anything. And as far as I know, my grandmother never even heard the gospel, she certainly wasn't going to be preaching it somewhere as anybody's "Missionary"). Finally, they had a prayer meeting and capped off the day with evening service. We usually arrived at 8:00 in the morning and were there sometimes until 9:00 or 10:00 at night.

The last time I remember my grandmother going to church was the time I caught the pastor in the closet of the choir rehearsal room having sex with one of the Missionary ladies.

I was playing hide-and-seek with some other kids on one of those all day Sundays and looking for a place to hide. I thought the robe closet in the choir rehearsal room would be the last place anyone would look and apparently so did the pastor and his companion.

When I swung the door open, there they were. We were all shocked and startled, and without thinking, the woman began to express her surprise by screaming. She just started screaming, so I started screaming and that brought the whole Missionary ladies meeting from across the hall into the room to see what all the screaming was about. And boy did they get an eyeful!

As many times as my grandmother, who was a very large woman, had pressed me into service to help her squeeze into her clothes, I had never seen someone trying to stuff so much into a girdle so small and trying to do it so fast!

> All the ladies, including the pastor's wife, were standing there staring, with their mouths hanging open.

The pastor was trying just as diligently to get his trousers adjusted, but neither of them was doing much more than inept fumbling. Meanwhile all the ladies from across the hall, including my grandmother and the pastor's wife, were standing there staring with their mouths hanging open.

That was the last time we ever went to that church and I know for a fact that the pastor and his wife were invited to leave town.

These are only anecdotes, not the examples by which all Christianity or believers in God should be judged or evaluated. And these examples certainly shouldn't be taken to deny that millions of *true Christians* in various denominations have authentic born again relationships

> My experience with *empty religion* began to shape my *mistaken* belief that God was not real.

with God through the shed blood of His only begotten Son Jesus Christ.

But I used these examples to point out how my experience with *empty religion* during a time in my life when I was vulnerable, victimized and very impressionable, began to shape my *mistaken* belief that God was not real or that people that said they knew Him, didn't really know much about Him at all.

The Doctrines of Demons

By the time I was an adult, I didn't believe anyone who claimed to speak for God actually did, not only because of my experiences as a child, but in large part also because of the time I spent as a very young man with the Nation of Islam, married to the oldest daughter of its leader, Louis Farrakhan.

I met Farrakhan's oldest daughter when I was seventeen years old; she was several years older. We fell in love and I was quickly drafted into the inner circle of her family which meant spending plenty of time with her father. About four years later, we were married by him in his home.

> I met Farrakhan's oldest daughter when I was seventeen years old.

I immediately found Louis Farrakhan to be a warm and brilliant man with a sharp wit, a welcoming smile, a playful nature and an ability to caress a violin as if he were born with it under his chin.

He once played for me personally after I complained of a headache. He had me lay down on his living room couch, took the instrument from its case and began to gently play the sweetest, most soothing and exquisite music I had ever heard.

I marveled at his ability, but also at the occasion of having the great Louis Farrakhan, fiery orator, controversial figure, world renowned leader of a religious organization that was known by followers as simply "The Nation," playing a finely crafted violin for the sole purpose of relieving my headache.

I marveled for a moment, but the music was so soothing and relaxing, that within minutes I was sound asleep. I rested like a baby and awakened refreshed and with the headache long gone. It truly impressed me.

When I first met Farrakhan, I had no idea who he was or why his daughter had initially insisted upon being so secretive about her last name and who she was. I thought she was being coy and mysterious.

It turned out that she was only being cautious. Her father had just recently emerged from seclusion. His rumored involvement in the assassination of Malcolm X and the backlash surrounding the revelations of womanizing and sexual and financial improprieties by the Nation of Islam's founder, Elijah Muhammad, had made Farrakhan quite unpopular and possibly put his life in jeopardy.

It was widely believed that Farrakhan had been the target of death plots for years. But now he was preparing to move back into the spotlight to take over "The Nation" and try to recapture the former strength of the organization that had been founded by his mentor.

The particular danger of this man's teaching and writing that I want to discuss here is the Nation of Islam's position on the Lord Jesus Christ.

In his rhetoric of the late seventies and early eighties, when I was close to him, Farrakhan would get crowds of primarily young, disenchanted, disenfranchised, and generally angry black men whipped into a frenzy with carefully constructed phrases. His oratory was designed to stimulate the baser human instincts of rage, resentment, and hatred and then direct them toward white people whom he convinced his crowds were literally the "devils" they should blame for their circumstances.

I had never been a racist and in its basic form racism didn't really make any sense to me. First of all, you have to abandon all reason to even consider the premise that people's social, emotional and moral characteristics are governed by the same biological factors that determine the shape of their features, the color of their skin and the texture of their hair.

I can't even believe we are still not very far removed from the ridiculous, yet once widely accepted, view that people who are brown are more apt to rob liquor stores while people who are pale are more apt to be honest and intelligent; the crazy premise that if you brown in the sun you're a thief, if you burn in the sun you're a thinker.

Or on the other end of the spectrum, Farrakhan's *equally* ridiculous brand of racism that through some miracle of ancient mystical manipulation of human DNA, "white devils" were cooked up from the genes that were spliced from black "Supermen."

At the depths of the doctrine Farrakhan adopted from Elijah Muhammad, where few converts actually delve, are the most outlandish and utterly foolish claims about Christ, the Bible, the origin of creation, salvation, science and technology that no reasonable, rational or even sane person could seriously consider.

Like for instance, that the moon is a chunk of the earth that was blown into space in an accidental explosion caused by the same ancient mad scientist responsible for cloning "white devils" from original black men.

But all of the Nation of Islam's doctrine, from the ridiculous to the sublime, completely denies and indeed rejects that the Lord Jesus Christ, the Son of God, by the shedding of

His blood has purchased the salvation of sinful man who is to be presented as a precious and purchased possession to a Holy God.

As a naïve young man, I admired Farrakhan because his oratory was thrilling; but as a wiser young man, I rejected him because his rhetoric was frightening. And it was not only outlandish, but completely focused on the flesh.

> It makes me shudder to see so many men turning their pulpits over to these doctrines of demons.

He had reduced all of the doctrines of the Almighty God, who is a Spirit, to petty considerations of the color of skin.

And yet today, the same spirit of useless *religion* that has mixed in paganism, people worship, statue worship, idolatry, powerless chanting and voodoo spells disguised as prayers and petitions, is also bringing this "Black Muslim" brand of crazy, Christ denying, soul-robbing, empty religious rhetoric into the pulpits of many of America's black churches.

It makes me shudder to see so many men who claim to be pastors of Christ turning their pulpits, in what are supposed to be houses of worship, over to these doctrines of demons.

The blasphemous rhetoric of Louis Farrakhan, which denies that Jesus is *the* Christ, *the* Savior of the world and *the* propitiation for sin by the shedding of His blood; that denies that Jesus is *the way, the truth, the life and that no one comes to the Father but through Him,* has regularly been invited and welcomed into the pulpits of so-called "Christian" churches to replace the life-giving, soul-saving gospel of the Lord Jesus

Christ!

It is a blasphemous crime and it must be stopped now. If you attend a church where the tenets and beliefs that were spawned by Muhammad or spread by Farrakhan are welcomed; or where any so-called "Black Muslim" is invited to do anything other than to fall on his knees at the cross of Christ to claim the covering of the blood of Jesus, then you should run away from it like it's on fire

I am not blaming Muhammad or Farrakhan for what the servants of satan masquerading as pastors of Christ have allowed; those "Black Muslim" men never kicked in the doors of any congregation to seize their church by the pulpit and force anything down their throats.

I'm laying the blame squarely on the heads of the pastors who have been blinded by empty *religion* and ignored the reality of Christ and who *willingly* threw open their doors and *invited* this abomination to be pumped into the hearts of their people.

The Moment of Truth

And so in order to cut through a lifetime of clutter left behind by the empty religion of my childhood, and the Nation of Islam's cultic nonsense in my young adulthood, the God who'd been talking to Nicky and me in my old apartment was about to speak again, but this time with the persuasion of power.

All of the false religion we had known; all of the futile and vain practices of our past that had threatened to keep us away from the truth, were about to be washed away in a flood of His glory and grace.

In the summer of 1999, Nicky and I had grown hungry for change, hungry for a new life, hungry for Jesus. We couldn't live without each other and she couldn't live with me the way I was.

We'd begun visiting the church of a friend who'd given us some cassettes of his pastor preaching about Christ. Our appetite was so voracious to hear more that we drove eighty-five miles each way from Lansing to Warren, Michigan to visit the congregation that was meeting in a school.

What we heard set our hearts on fire and burned in our brains. We bought a tape of the first message we heard there and listened to it again on the way home. I told Nicky that I had wanted to respond to the altar call at the end of the service, but fear and embarrassment kept me in my seat.

I thought that everybody in the service must've known about all my troubles and I was too self conscious and worried about what other people would say and think about me.

> We had been disappointed by religion, but we both knew this was different.

But I told Nicky that I wanted to go back the following Sunday. She told me that she was already thinking the same thing. She had been in church most of her life; we both had been either unmoved or disappointed by religion, but we both knew this was different.

It seemed like it took the next Sunday forever to finally

arrive. We were so excited about returning, not only to hear more about the Lord, but to feel the manifest presence we had experienced before.

There's No High Like The Most High

When Sunday came, we arrived at the church with great anticipation. The service was again moving and powerful. The preaching about Christ had illuminated my mind, softened my heart and resolved my conviction. If I could have balled myself up into my own hand, I would have thrown myself at Jesus.

He was willing to catch what the world was trying to throw away. All that I could give Him was a drug addicted alcoholic; a man not only fired and unemployed but unemployable, destroyed in body, mind and reputation; a man humiliated and broken. And yet, Jesus still wanted me. I could not run to Him fast enough.

> All that I could give Him was a man humiliated and broken. And yet, Jesus still wanted me.

At the end of the service, when the call was made to come to the altar, I responded without hesitation. The pastor leaned down to whisper in my ear, but instead of his voice, I heard the echo of thunder, like my head had once again become the cavernous chamber of the Lord's visitation in my old apartment.

But this time, a sizzle shot through my body and knocked me to my knees. A few minutes later when I could pull myself together and pull myself up off the floor (with the help of several people) I vowed that this would be no passing experience. I was going to grab onto God by the feet of Jesus and never let go.

> ## In that moment, I belonged to Jesus.

In that moment, I believed. In that moment, I was His. In that moment, I belonged to Jesus. I knew that His blood had been shed for me and I knew that in the same way His tomb was empty, no grave would ever be my final resting place.

I wasn't sure about the "how" but I was sure about Heaven. At the time, I wasn't technically sure what qualified someone to authentically be called a Christian, but looking back, I am sure that was the moment in which I was born again.

Breaking Away from the Pack

By Sunday August 1, 1999, I'd been sober for months and we had been regularly attending the church since June. I was still craving drugs and alcohol; but by then, I was determined not to get high on anything but the presence of Jesus Christ. Even though I was relying on my willpower instead of God's power through the Holy Spirit to stay straight, it was good to feel free.

Nicky, her children and I were headed to church as usual; but this Sunday, to me, was special. This was the day that I was determined to be free from my addiction to cigarettes.

Nicky was so pleased that I was sober, she was content to

continue to let me smoke without pressure. In her mind, though, she had always determined that she would never marry a smoker, which made what would happen that weekend all the more miraculous.

Still filling in at the radio station, I had told my colleagues on that Friday that when they next saw me on Monday, I would no longer be a smoker. For twenty-five years, I had been infamous as a smoker. Over that time, I smoked no less than a pack a day except for the briefest attempts at quitting.

My attempts were so brief and always unsuccessful because I would become so unbearable. I'd suffer from paralyzing headaches and sleep disturbing bed-drenching night-sweats. I'd get moody and irritable and generally become such a pain that if I didn't go back to smoking, my friends and co-workers would buy cigarettes for me.

Someone told me once that they'd rather visit me in the cancer ward than be around me one more day trying to quit.

But week after week during prayer in that service we kept visiting, the pastor would say that in the presence of Jesus was the place to enlarge your requests. And so I had determined that this was the time I was going to be set free from the bondage of addiction to nicotine.

I was so confident that the Lord would hear and honor my petition that I gleefully told everyone at the radio station that my deliverance from smoking cigarettes by the power of the Lord Jesus Christ was coming that Sunday.

Until then, the prospect of never smoking again made me

want to smoke more than ever. From Friday to Sunday morning I smoked more fiendishly than ever in my twenty-five years of addiction. But I laughed it off. In my mind, I told the cigarettes in my pocket, "You have me now, but in a matter of hours I'll be free of you forever!"

> I told the cigarettes in my pocket, "In a matter of hours I'll be free of you forever!"

When prayer time in the service came, I was tingling with excitement. The presence of God, the power of God, the glory of God were filling the sanctuary, and there was great anticipation that a move of God would bring healing and deliverance to many of the people there.

I silently prayed the petition I'd been waiting since Friday, indeed for twenty-five years actually, to make. I felt so alive, so wonderful, *so much like running right out that moment and having a cigarette*! I couldn't believe it. I wasn't free. If anything I was craving a cigarette more than ever!

I told myself that the craving was a shadow that was only in my mind; that I was free from cigarettes and that as soon as I came to the realization of what had been done for me, I would feel the results.

I tried to stop thinking about smoking as we enjoyed what turned out to be another powerful service and we praised and worshipped the Lord with gladness. Our new life was blossoming more fully each week. I still couldn't bear to hear or see anything about cocaine use in a movie or TV show and sometimes just hearing the word gave me a shudder. But I was holding out and holding on.

Near the end of the service, I had a vision that at first seemed like a daydream. I could see Nicky and me standing at the front of the church right at the end of the service being married by the pastor!

I heard the Holy Spirit say, "See? Just like that."

I was sure that Nicky had heard it because it was so loud and clear. I turned to her and said, "Yeah, just like that!"

She looked at me and said, "Just like what? What are you talking about?"

I said, "Didn't you hear that?" as it began to dawn on me that only I had heard that voice in my mind. But I knew that God was telling me that the time had come, and it was safe to make Nicky my wife.

I couldn't let her marry a drug addict, and He wouldn't either. I couldn't let her marry a smoker, and God didn't plan to either. Even though I still felt the craving, He was telling me I could still plan the wedding and that it should be a simple little ceremony at the end of a regular Sunday service like this one.

> When I finally came right out and asked Nicky to marry me, she was stunned.

"Just like that," I said again, half to Nicky and half mumbling to myself. She had no idea what I was talking about.

When I finally came right out and asked Nicky to marry

me, she was stunned, and at first didn't really believe I was serious. I told her that I thought we should do it very soon and very simply. I told her about the small ceremony in my vision and explained that it was what the "just like that" thing was all about.

Proposing a simple, no frills, quickly thrown together wedding to take place right at the end of a Sunday service, at the altar of a church that meets in a school, is not something that would thrill most women.

But Nicky is not like most women. In fact, when it comes to certain things like simplicity and sincerity, she is unlike any woman I have ever known.

It was the *marriage* that was on her mind, not the *wedding*; *that* we would get married took precedence over *how* we would get married; the covenant we were planning to last a lifetime was more urgent than planning the ceremony that would only last a few minutes.

We had talked about marriage from the moment we met, which was remarkable since the selling point that made our initial meeting attractive was that it was a casual and meaningless blind date.

I never had any doubt about my intentions toward her from the beginning, and Nicky had always let me know that except for the whole, *depressed, unemployed, drug addict* thing, I was the man of her dreams.

I believe she said yes mostly because she could see the dramatic impact being in the presence of the Lord was having on both our lives, mine in particular, and partly because saying yes was harmless if I wasn't really serious, which she wasn't sure I was.

We set the date right there for Sunday, August twenty-second. We had planned to be baptized together on the Sunday before our wedding, so that we could begin our new lives together as publicly declared new creations in Christ.

We were both thrilled and excited over our plans and the new life together that we were trying to envision. I could hardly believe all that had changed so much in just over a year. When I had first met Nicky, I knew she was my future; as we grew closer, it was like I couldn't breathe without her and this woman who had become the air I needed had just agreed to give me an unlimited supply for the rest of our lives.

> I couldn't breathe without her and this woman who had become the air I needed had just agreed to give me an unlimited supply.

Again, I thought *Wow. What a woman.*

When we left church after that service, I had the woman of my dreams as my fiancée, but still had nicotine as my addiction and I kept trying to ignore the craving to smoke, but it continued. I couldn't wait to get a couple blocks away from the church, roll down the windows and light up. I was ashamed and embarrassed that I hadn't received the deliverance I'd been so sure would come.

That evening at home I continued to go out on the deck of

our condo to smoke, and went through almost the entire pack.

The next day as I was driving to the radio station in Southfield, I was finishing the last cigarette in the pack I'd practically emptied the day before. I was already dreading my arrival at the station because I knew people would ask what happened with the smoking prayer.

I decided I would just tell the truth. I prayed, I expected, nothing happened. That's a very sad testimony, I thought, but it's the truth.

I've since learned that the Lord says when you pray for His help, that you have to believe you receive what you ask for *when* you pray. I believed at first, but then when I didn't feel the results at the time I expected, I began to doubt.

> There is no more powerful prayer, than praying God's own Words back to Him.

As I flicked the butt of my last smoke out of the car window, I faced a choice: whether to stop for cigarettes, or try to quit again on my own.

I began to talk out loud to the Lord and I was praying His Word back to Him without out even knowing it. There is no more powerful prayer than praying God's own Words back to Him.

I told the Lord that I simply was not going to smoke. That I was going to sacrifice my body to Him and that no matter how much I suffered as a result, I would prove that I could live for His glory. I told God that if I suffered nicotine withdrawal as I had in the past, that I would let it remind me of His suffering for me and consider it an honor.

Without even knowing it, I was repeating the Word of God from Romans Chapter 12:

> I beseech you therefore, brethren, by the mercies of God, that you present your bodies a living sacrifice, holy, acceptable to God, *which is* your reasonable service. And do not be conformed to this world, but be transformed by the renewing of your mind, that you may prove what is that good and acceptable and perfect will of God (Romans 12:1–2).

God's Word says that if you present your body as a living sacrifice in response to His mercy, then you will be able to prove, or test, what His perfect will for your life is. God's perfect will for your life is always for you to be free: free from pain, sickness, disease, sin, death, poverty and bondage of *every* kind.

> When I prayed that prayer, it ignited something I could have never imagined.

When I prayed that prayer, offering my body as a sacrifice to serve the Lord and be a temple of the Holy Spirit where the pollution of cigarette smoke would no longer be allowed, no matter what the suffering, it lined up perfectly with the Word of God, and it ignited something I could have never imagined.

Right in that moment as I was driving down the highway

from Lansing to Southfield, the glory of God filled my vehicle and the manifest presence and power of the Lord was so strong and so heavy, that my eyes blurred, tears filled them and began to stream down my face. I couldn't even see where I was going but I knew the power of God had taken over my vehicle and I was convinced that nothing bad could happen to me.

The Lord's presence was so strong that it was almost like I could actually see Him in the passenger seat of the car reaching His hand over to my chest. And in that moment I felt a pressure, about the size of a man's hand, pressing hard against my chest, which suddenly felt warm, even hot and tingled as the pressure increased.

And then it subsided as if the hand was gone. The warm tingling sensation ceased. I was very aware of being in control of the vehicle again, and I was also very aware of something else. I no longer had any desire to smoke.

But it wasn't as if the desire was simply overcome or even had been removed. It was and has been as if I had never smoked a cigarette nor had ever been addicted to nicotine at all. It was suddenly like I had *never smoked*!

When I pulled into the radio station parking lot, I was bursting! I wanted to run and shout the name of Jesus! I wanted to jump up and down and scream at the top of my lungs, Jesus! Jesus! Jesus!

At the time, I didn't have nearly the boldness I would begin to have even months later, let alone now. I wanted to tell everyone exactly what happened, but I was afraid of what their reaction would be and I knew they wouldn't believe me.

Before I went into the building, I coughed and a bit of fluid flew out of my mouth from my lungs. Over the years as a smoker I had coughed up a lot of stuff from my lungs; most of it was black or brown or greenish yellow at best (sorry), but when I looked on the ground, I knew my lungs had been repaired.

The fluid that had come up was completely *clear.* Throughout the day, my co-workers at the radio station asked me how the weekend went and how that "prayer thing" with the cigarettes turned out.

I gleefully, but calmly, told each one that it turned out well. I was free.

Several years later, an examination to evaluate lung capacity, called a Spirometry, confirmed what I had already known. The damage to my lungs had been completely healed!

The damage from twenty-five years of smoking no less than a pack of cigarettes every day, the damage from smoking no less than

> The damage of twenty-five years of smoking had been completely healed.

a half ounce of high-grade marijuana every week and the damage from smoking hundreds of thousands of dollars worth of pure cocaine for up to six days at a time without ceasing for twenty-two years, had been completely healed in my lungs which were not only restored, but improved!

Based on the data my doctor entered into his computer to calculate the capacity of my lungs, I have much more lung capacity than I should! Hallelujah!

You Say Goodbye and I Say Hello

Suddenly, miraculously and completely delivered from smoking, I was in shock. It was wonderful, it was thrilling, and it was the greatest freedom I had ever experienced.

Twenty-five years of lighting, puffing, and flicking away ashes; twenty-five years of brown fingertips, stinking breath and generally smelling like an ashtray from my clothing to my hair; twenty-five years of craving, coughing, and serving the twenty slave masters in every pack was over in an instant with one miraculous touch of the Lord's loving hand.

It was wonderful and what made it even better was that I had no withdrawal or urges; in fact, I had an immediate and severe aversion to even the smell of cigarette smoke which now completely nauseates me.

And it also meant that Nicky was getting another desire of *her* heart: a husband who was not a smoker.

When she had pledged in her mind *that she would never marry a smoker*, and believed God would give her the desires of her heart and then agreed to marry me while I *was* a smoker, she was standing on faith that God could turn her desire into my deliverance.

Our wedding day seemed to be approaching so fast, especially now that my wife-to-be had finally wrapped her mind around the certainty that in just over two weeks she was going to be married.

Nicky hadn't put much concentration into preparing for the wedding, which was unusual for her, given the extreme focus she can bring to making an event or occasion happen. She has the ability to turn her attention into a laser that can cut through any obstacle to completing a task or project or making an event successful.

Finally, she told me that she had slacked on the preparations because part of her had still been hesitant to believe it was all really happening. It was not that long ago that she was seriously about to dump me in spite of being incredibly in love with me, because my life was such a mess. But in her faithfulness to the Lord, even though at that time she did not actually have a personal relationship with Him, she made a commitment.

And now, almost overnight it seemed, I was sane and sober, delivered from my smoking addiction, employed at least part-time, we were in church every Sunday morning for service and Tuesday nights for Bible study and planning to be married!

> It was like the old Frank Turner was disappearing right in front of her eyes.

It was all wonderful, but it just didn't seem possible. It was overwhelming. It was like the old Frank Turner was disappearing bit by bit right in front of her eyes and an entirely new man was emerging to introduce himself.

Because our plans were simple and our invited guests were few, we were able to put most of our concentration into selecting rings. We needed to find something affordable (which meant something that was *nothing* like the ring I wanted to give her) and we also wanted to get wedding bands for her teenaged son and daughter.

Our new blended family was going to be a bit of a challenge and we wanted the children to feel and know that I was marrying them as well as their mother. We all talked about it and they thought the idea of getting wedding bands also, as their mother and I exchanged rings, would be a wonderful experience.

When Nicky and I first met, we agreed it should be a while before I met her children Andrea and Austin. There was no sense in bringing home something casual to the kids. But our relationship became rather serious rather fast and very soon after Nicky and I realized we were very much in love, the children and I started forming a relationship of our own.

But, it was complicated. First of all, their time was divided between their mother's household and their dad's. That meant they were constantly shifting between two sets of rules and patterns and the different atmospheres of the different households.

Secondly, I was a complete stranger with some difficult *issues* and then suddenly—I was moving into their mother's condominium which was barely big enough to accommodate them, *plus* I was bringing a ton of stuff *and* my dog Ginger with me.

And to top it all off, right in the middle of them trying to get acquainted with the smoking, drinking, cussing, trashy movie loving, dirty joke telling Frank Turner, I suddenly started getting delivered from all that; *and* they're mother and I began packing them off to church every week!

And when I say church, I'm not talking about anything like the old dried up, dead, stale *religious* church they had been used to for most of their lives; we were spending our time at a full-blown, fired up, full gospel, Pentecostal church where the Holy Spirit would light you up and the power of God would knock you down.

They seemed to love going to the church and had some wonderful experiences, still it was a lot for the twelve and thirteen

Frank and Nicky's wedding day, 1999.

year olds to take in. We had our share of tension at times, but they rolled with the program changes very well and we have always loved each other while we learned to adjust to the dramatic shift in all of our lives.

> Nobody was looking for the death that was going to happen at the baptism.

The biggest shift came a week before the one we were all expecting which was the wedding. While we all had our sights set on the new life that would begin with the marriage, nobody was looking for the death that was going to happen at the baptism.

This brings us back to that pool at Greater Apostolic Faith Church in Detroit On August 15, 1999 where Nicky and I were being baptized. The pool was in the baptistry above the altar. We were there because the church in Warren where we had heard and believed the gospel and trusted Christ for our salvation did not have a pool of its own.

Come Forth

I was so excited and felt like I was on fire—blazing from the inside out and I could not wait to be immersed in the water. In a dressing room just off the pool I had changed out of my clothes into one of the white baptismal outfits they kept for visitors. It had never occurred to me to bring something special of my own to be baptized in. Looking back I wish I had so I could have saved it as a keepsake.

There were separate dressing rooms on either side of the baptistry so that men and women could have privacy. I could neither see nor hear Nicky and I wondered what was happening over on her side.

When I was led out into the pool, the music was loud. The praise team which was right below the baptistry was singing and my head was spinning and my heart racing. The nearly waist-high water was slightly cool, but it felt wonderful and I could see everybody in the congregation looking up toward the baptistry.

I had three things on my mind: the first, of course was Jesus. Then I wondered what Nicky was doing and whether she had been immersed yet. And I was also wondering why, at that particular moment, the urge for cocaine which I had been fighting for about three months was suddenly irresistible.

> I was wondering why the urge for cocaine was suddenly irresistible.

It was as if right in that moment, just before my public declaration of my love for and allegiance to the Lord Jesus Christ, satan was taking one last shot at exploiting my vulnerability for that drug. And the power of my will that had been sufficient to that point was not enough. I needed the power of the Grace of God.

I can honestly say that as much as I loved the Lord in that moment, if someone had passed a torch and a pipe with a bowl full of "rock" to me right at that second, I probably would have taken a hit.

Only now can I see that in that moment in the baptismal pool, the Lord was taking me back to the moment of His visitation in my bedroom, the night He saved me from my third heart attack and fatal overdose, the night He extended His hand and gave me an ultimatum I could not meet.

> The Lord gave me one last chance to look at bondage in hell before He set me free.

I had been helpless over that drug then and I was helpless again right in this moment, standing in that pool waiting to be

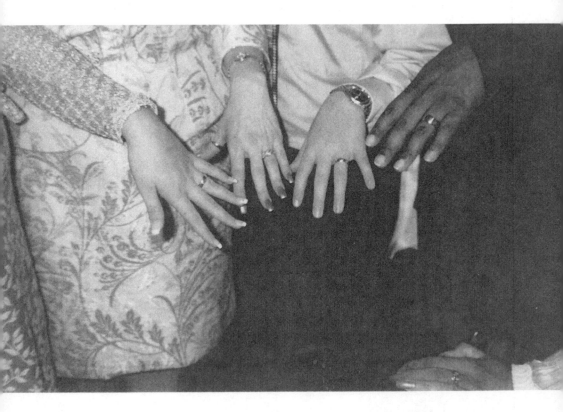

Andrea, Nicky, Austin and Frank "band" together, 1999.

immersed in the blood of Christ, to be buried in the tomb of Christ, to let the old Frank Turner die and see the new Frank Turner rise up and walk in the newness of life filled with the spirit of Christ.

It was time for everybody in this world to say goodbye to him and say hello to a new me.

But on the way out of this life, the Lord also wanted that Frank Turner to know that he was dying as the slave he'd been born. Frank Turner had been a child of the devil and a slave to sin. Frank Turner was in bondage to heartache

Frank Turner was a stone cold cocaine junkie crack-head.

and pain, disappointment and death; Frank Turner had been the slave of obsessions and urges, lusts and passions; Frank Turner was a stone cold cocaine junkie crack-head who, if left to his own devices, decisions and strength, would end up right back in the pit wallowing around in death and destruction until he killed everything in his path and everything in his life.

And that is why he had to die. The Lord didn't come to tame the flesh or train the flesh; He took on the likeness of sinful flesh, yet without sin so that He could become sin for us. He became sin in the flesh for us, so that He could take our sinful flesh to the cross...and kill it.

But before I died, He wanted me to have one last taste of who I really was, one last look at a man in chains, one last urge to run back into the bondage which had destroyed my mind, my body, my career and my life, one last look at the man I'd seen in the mirror in my apartment on his knees. The Lord gave me one last chance to take a good look at bondage in hell, before He set me free in the Kingdom of God.

The Lord wanted me to have a moment of assurance that would make me completely free from doubt, free from the influence of unbelievers and free from any chance of failure, free to go on as a new man with no fear of ever looking over my shoulder and seeing the old one.

And then it was right in that moment when that big strong deacon who was in the pool with me, crossed my forearms over my chest and held them there, put his other hand firmly against my back and tilted me backwards until I was completely immersed.

> The Lord Jesus ordered me to "Come forth!" and in that instant everything changed.

As I was being immersed in the baptismal pool; in that brief moment that I was being held under the water, thirty-three years of pain and heartache and anxiety and depression; twenty-five years of drug and alcohol addiction including twenty-two years spent helplessly and hopelessly addicted to smoking pure cocaine, suddenly and miraculously **DISAPPEARED**. It was all snatched right out of me by the hand of the Lord Jesus Christ!

As He had done at the grave of Lazarus, the Lord Jesus called into the tomb of the man being buried beneath the surface of that water and ordered me to "Come forth!" and in that instant, everything changed.

My mind and body were healed, my addiction was broken and my heart was filled with the Spirit of God.

As I was lifted out of the water, I was screaming like a new baby at birth. I knew from those last moments of bondage which I had been allowed to realize as a gift from God that in this moment of new birth I was, in an instant, *free forever*.

The addiction that had once again painted the taste of cocaine across my tongue just seconds earlier, was broken, crushed and destroyed in a single instant.

And also in that moment, my heart, which like my lungs, had been irreparably damaged by a quarter century of drug abuse, was immediately, miraculously and completely healed and restored by the divine touch of the Lord Jesus Christ Himself. Hallelujah! Glory to God!

People often ask me, how I knew right in that moment that I was free. Trust me, when you have been struggling under the weight of a massive burden that has finally crushed you into the dust like a fine powder, you know the instant it has been taken off your back. I knew I was free and while subsequent tests have confirmed the soundness of my heart, I knew in that moment that I was healed.

Several weeks later, alone in my bedroom, I was baptized again; but this time there was no water. In a glorious moment alone with God, I was immersed in the Holy Spirit and His presence began to completely fill me, wash over me and bubble over and spill out of me, and I began to speak in tongues as The Spirit gave utterance.

Yes, I'm one of *those* people.

I climbed out of that pool August 15, 1999, a new man. I went into the water believing that the Lord Jesus Christ was my Savior, but it was something about the commitment I was making to Him by being baptized that day that brought the realization of the fullness of His healing, deliverance and restoring power into my life.

Every believer, if possible, should be baptized, and I have heard other wonderful testimonies of miracles the Lord has performed while people were in the baptismal pool.

But I don't really think it was the baptism *per se* that had anything to do with the deliverance and healing. I don't believe it was the moment in the water, I believe it was the moment itself; the moment of joining, the moment of release and surrender; the moment when I said to the Lord, "Take me,

> "Take me, I am nothing without you, I cannot go on without you."

I am helpless without you; I am nothing without you; I cannot go on without you."

That was the answer the Lord had asked of me that night in my apartment when he told me to abandon the drugs and follow Him; the answer that until He set me free from the bondage of addiction, I had not been free to give.

In that moment of realization of my helplessness and surrender to His control and power by faith, I received the yoke destroying power of His anointing. That's what "Christ" means: *The Anointed One.* And in that moment of surrender, I received the fullness of *The Anointed One* **AND** *His Anointing.*

I changed back into my clothes as quickly as I could and went down to the sanctuary to find Nicky. I couldn't wait to discover how her baptism had gone, what had happened and how she felt. I wondered how she would receive my report and whether I would even be able to put into words right in that moment the fullness of what had just happened.

I was so elated and it was hard to calm down even enough to hold still. There was so much going on and so many people around us that it was several hours before we could be alone and have a discussion in depth about the details of our special day.

It was the day the world said goodbye to the old me and the new me said hello.

The Resurrection and the Life

Now Martha said to Jesus, "Lord, if You had been here, my brother would not have died" (John 11:21).

Imagine that. Martha (and probably many others) thought Jesus had arrived too late! "If only you had gotten here sooner," she told Him. The Lord that Martha believed could save Lazarus from illness was not the one she believed could raise him from the dead.

So now that Jesus had arrived, rather than meet Him with rejoicing, relief and glee, Martha met Him with a complaint. If only He had come sooner.

I too, at times, have reacted to the saving grace of the Lord Jesus Christ with a complaint veiled as a question. "Why didn't you come sooner?"

"Why didn't you come sooner Lord, before I was abandoned and abused, before I was addicted and destroyed, before the two divorces and the pair of bankruptcies, before the public firing and complete humiliation? Why didn't you come sooner Lord, before the death of my parents orphaned me, before the molesters raped me and the demons encircled me, before the drugs, alcohol, nicotine and pornography trapped me, before sin enslaved me? Sooner, Lord, why didn't you come sooner?"

> Why didn't you come sooner Lord, before sin enslaved me?

If we are to trust the Lord, we must first trust His timing. Secondly, we must trust that as He arrives at the perfect time, He is able to do *anything*; even "...exceedingly abundantly above all that we ask or think..." (Ephesians 3:20).

Have you ever reacted to the Lord this way? Have you ever begged for heavenly assistance? Have you ever pleaded for God to step into your circumstances and then scoffed at His help as coming too late?

Sometimes, as in the case with Martha, our reaction is more about unbelief than being ungrateful. When the Lord isn't operating according to our timetable, we have trouble believing He can solve our problems or meet our needs. While we *say* we trust Him, often our level of trust decreases in direct proportion to the time we spend waiting to see the answer to our prayers.

How easily we forget that while God answers our prayers for *our* good, ultimately the purpose of His answer is for *His* glory. The entirety of Jesus' ministry has been service to our good and God's glory!

All Things Work Together for Good

None of what the Lord has done with our ministry would have been possible had it not been for the gifts bestowed upon Nicky and me in the summer of 1999, particularly on August fifteenth.

The Lord Jesus Christ called me to salvation, deliverance, healing and restoration on that wonderful day.

And now, through this testimony, He is calling the world. He rolled away the stone of my tomb to show the world that he can reach into the darkest region of death, into the strongest stench of failure and transgression, grab a hold of the filthiest refuse and by the power of His call, speak life into death.

> He can reach into the strongest stench of failure and speak life into death.

In the summer of 1999, a gravestone was rolled away and the stench of death filled the air. That smell was my life exactly as I've candidly described for you on these pages.

When I was a child, I was abandoned, abused and turned out into the world. With no where else to turn in this life, I eventually turned to the "high life" and by the age of fourteen, drugs had become my refuge. By the age of seventeen, addictions had become my bondage.

I spent twenty-five years convincing myself that a chemical hell was a place of shelter, that poison was medicine, and that death was the only escape.

Twice, I melted everything I owned into a crack pipe and threw myself into financial ruin. I smoked myself into two bankruptcies, two divorces, and three fatal heart attacks.

I smoked myself out of every meaningful relationship and out of several television jobs I had to leave just to stay a few steps ahead of being fired.

And finally, I smoked myself out of the pinnacle of my success, the height of my career, the single most important, prestigious and highest paying position for which I had worked my entire life.

In the final drug induced irony, I had used my six figure income to finance what had in the end become a $4,000 a week cocaine addiction that left me too incapacitated to show up for the job and collect the paycheck that was financing my addiction.

The stone has been rolled away so that you can be assured that no matter where you've been or what you've been through, I have been there with you.

That smell from my tomb is the odor of the destroyed life of Frank Turner.

Frank Turner has been unwanted, unneeded, unloved and unnoticed.

Frank Turner has been lost, lonely and alone with nowhere to turn and no one to turn to.

Frank Turner has been beaten, broken, abused and assaulted.

Frank Turner has been violated, molested and raped.

Frank Turner has been addicted, enslaved, trapped and imprisoned.

I have stumbled, failed and fallen; I have crushed, damaged and destroyed; I have wasted, wrecked and ruined.

> I have been where you've been and suffered every hurt you've suffered.

I have been wherever you've been; done everything you've done and suffered every hurt you've suffered.

And it all brought me to this place, down on my knees, where I could stretch out my hand and beg you to come and follow me to where the healing is.

On August 15, 1999, I stepped into a baptismal pool to publicly devote my life to the Savior who had publicly borne my sin. He met me there and changed my life forever.

His same healing hand is stretched out to you now. Will you take it? All you have to do is believe. My life is an extension of Christ's love, mercy and healing to you. I am an example of all that He wants to do in your life.

The Lord wants you to be saved, delivered, healed, healthy and whole. He restored my life, my name, my career and reputation. He has blessed us with our wonderful daughters, Ally and Rachel, and my wife's children, Andrea and Austin.

The Lord Jesus Christ reached into the mire of helpless pain, addiction, filthy degradation and death to pull me out. He has blessed our lives in every possible realm: spiritually, emotionally, psychologically, physically, financially and materially. All you have to do is believe.

Jesus Christ stood outside the tomb of Lazarus and declared that he had only been allowed to die so that he could be raised up and used as an example so that *unbelievers* would become *believers*.

CHAPTER NINE

WHAT IT MEANS TO BE BORN AGAIN

Jesus answered and said to him, "Most assuredly,
I say to you, unless one is born again, he
cannot see the kingdom of God"
(John 3:3).

Friends, I cannot emphasize what I'm about to say strongly enough. There is a heavy and pervasive spirit of *religion* that has penetrated the church and by its subtle and sinister hypnotic attraction, it is leading thousands into a fatal reliance on false doctrines, empty and vain ritualistic practices, futile traditions of self-righteousness, and a culture of paganism emerging in our pews.

The only true, *God-given* system for man to practice was the Theocracy of the Kingdom of God given to the nation of Israel. But the required obedience to God's laws, statutes and judgments could never bring redemption from sin or be followed to the standard of perfection required by God for righteousness.

> The shedding of blood is still the only avenue for the forgiveness of sin.

And the blood sacrifices of animals once used to make up for the shortcomings of the children of Israel under the law of Moses are no longer being accepted and cannot be offered to God.

But the shedding of blood is still the only avenue for the forgiveness of sin:

> And according to the law almost all things are
> purified with blood, and without shedding of blood
> there is no remission (Hebrews 9:22).

There is only one sacrifice of blood available to mankind today for the forgiveness of sin and that is the blood shed by the Lord Jesus Christ on His cross.

> But this Man, after He had offered one sacrifice
> for sins forever, sat down at the right hand of
> God, from that time waiting till His enemies are
> made His footstool. For by one offering He has
> perfected forever those who are being sanctified
> (Hebrews 10:12–14).

There is only one salvation and that is the salvation of receiving the righteousness of God through faith in His Son Jesus Christ.

There is no self-righteousness. There is only the righteousness of God and the righteousness of God is the Lord Jesus Christ. The Lord said you must be born again to enter or even see the kingdom of God. To be born again means to be born of the Spirit; to be born of God.

Everyone who believes that Jesus is the Christ is born of God, and everyone who loves the father loves his child as well (1 John 5:1).

A person cannot be born again without belief in Christ. But to be born again involves more than just the reciting of a Christian "Pledge of Allegiance." The single greatest injustice in the Church today is telling people that just because they recite some so-called "Sinner's Prayer" or "Prayer of Salvation," that means they are saved.

> A person cannot be born again without belief in Christ.

DO NOT BE MISLED. IT IS A MATTER OF LIFE AND DEATH. YOU CANNOT *PRAY* YOUR WAY TO SALVATION; YOU MUST BE BORN AGAIN.

Nothing in the Bible says that salvation is obtained by prayer. Nor should anyone be fooled into thinking that being led in the reciting of a prayer and "...really believing what you just said..." as the now standard line goes, results in being born again.

Come, let us reason together. Let us be both logical and Biblical since the Bible is the revelation of God who is the very source of wisdom and order.

If reciting the so-called "Prayer of Salvation" resulted in being born again and saved, then everyone who recited it would be saved and born again. Obviously, that isn't the case.

In fact, the vast majority of people who are led in the

recitation of the "Sinner's Prayer" or "Prayer of Salvation" at the altars of American churches never even return a second time to the church where they supposedly "confessed unto salvation."

Confession does not cause salvation; salvation causes confession. You do not create belief in your heart by confessing with your mouth; you create confession in your mouth by what you believe in your heart!

> **Confession does not cause salvation; salvation causes confession.**

Confessing your faith as a prayer confirms your salvation only if you really have trusted Christ by faith in a born again heart.

You must first receive the new heart that is promised in the new covenant because your old heart, the seat of your old carnal sinful nature is not capable of accepting and believing the spiritual truth of Christ.

> But the natural man does not receive the things of the Spirit of God, for they are foolishness to him; nor can he know *them*, because they are spiritually discerned (1 Corinthians 2:14).

Therefore, when one is confessing with his mouth the Lord Jesus Christ, it is because he *believes* in his *new heart* that God has raised Him from the dead. Now, his confession is *confirming* his salvation.

Also, and perhaps **most importantly**, most of the recitations of the so-called "Prayer of Salvation" that I have witnessed involved absolutely no mention whatsoever of the Lord's resurrection.

These prayers usually go something like this:

Lord Jesus, I confess that I am a sinner worthy of death and an eternal punishment in hell. I repent of my sin. I believe that You died for me, and because of the shedding of Your blood, I am forgiven. I invite You into my heart now and I ask You to forgive me. I ask You to save me Lord Jesus. Show me how to go forward, living for You. Amen.

There are as many variations of this prayer as there are altars where people are being led to recite it, but what they all have in common is that there is rarely, if ever, any mention of the empty tomb from which Christ has risen from the dead.

This is astounding because supposedly these prayers are based on the "confession" of Romans 10:9–10 which clearly states that the confessor is required to believe *that Jesus has been raised from the dead*:

[T]hat if you confess with your mouth the Lord Jesus and believe in your heart that God has raised Him from the dead, you will be saved (Romans 10:9).

The Resurrection is of co-equal importance with the Crucifixion because it is the Resurrection that confirms that the Crucifixion has satisfied God through the propitiation (the atoning sacrifice, the complete payment, the full satisfaction to which nothing can be added) of Jesus' blood.

It is not enough to believe merely *that Jesus has risen* as some corners of Christendom do. To be saved, you must believe in *why Jesus has risen:*

> who was delivered up because of our offenses,
> and was raised because of our justification
> (Romans 4:25).

Notice in particular that He "...*was raised because of our justification.*"

The born again heart believes not only that Jesus has risen, but that the empty tomb is the sign of the justification by the new covenant in Christ's blood. The new covenant is not just for our forgiveness, but also for our justification. It means we are declared righteous before God.

We are righteous because righteousness has been accounted or *imputed* to us in the same way that the Lord was able to *become sin for us. Sin was accounted or imputed to Him.*

Jesus was not actually a sinner or sinful, but *sin was accounted to Him and He was judged as if it was His own.* We are not actually righteous, *but righteousness is accounted or imputed to us, and we are considered as if it is our own*; therefore, we are justified before God.

Not only must we believe that Jesus is Lord and believe that He died and shed His blood for our sins, but we must also believe that Jesus has risen from the grave *because* we are **justified** and declared righteous.

> The confession is meant to be a statement that actually confirms that salvation has taken place.

In other words: you *are* righteous because—by faith in the truth of what Jesus Christ has actually done—you *believe* you are righteous.

Once this belief has been apprehended by your new heart, then your confession confirms your salvation; whether or not it takes the form of the so-called "Sinner's Prayer" or "Prayer of Salvation" or some other valid confession.

> For with the heart a person believes (adheres to, trusts in, and relies on Christ) and so is justified (declared righteous, acceptable to God), and with the mouth he confesses (declares openly and speaks out freely his faith) and confirms [his] salvation (Romans 10:10, AMP).

You see, the confession is not a prayer to recite that brings about salvation, the confession is meant to be a statement that actually confirms that salvation has taken place.

So in a sense, it is true that if a person has "…said these

words and meant them" that the person is saved. But the question is: what do the words *mean* to this individual?

If the words are the indication of what has actually transpired in the heart, then they are a confirmation. If the words are merely a statement of what the person thinks *sounds good at the time, has been talked into*, or *thinks is just the right thing to say because everybody is looking*, then it is a false confession.

The problem in America is that we are so focused on *closing the deal, chalking up* a salvation, or *filling a seat* in a church with a "new believer," that often no distinction is made between the confirmation of the truly saved and the false confession of the pretender.

Heaven is not a club that can be joined by reciting an oath. The confession must be a *confession of faith*.

Being born again requires your belief. That is your part. But it also requires several actions from God which He promised in the New Covenant in Christ's blood.

> Therefore, if anyone *is* in Christ, *he is* a new
> creation; old things have passed away; behold, all
> things have become new (2 Corinthians 5:17).

There are several promises of the new birth in Christ that are summed up in the Apostle Paul's statement. He tells us that a person in Christ is ...*a new creation*...and that ...*old things have passed away*... and that ...*all things have become new.*

The assurance of these statements is that being "born

again" (John 3:3–7) is much more than the adoption of a religious practice; it is secured by God Himself, and it involves a real and substantial change in your entire being.

Let's consider the promises of what it means to be a "new creation."

Believers in Christ are truly new creations. God actually takes you as the person you were from your first "natural" birth and then *re-creates* you through the spiritual new birth of faith in Christ. This means there are dramatic differences between the old and new.

> Believers in Christ are new creations. God actually *re-creates* you through Christ.

First of all, a born again person will not only see, but enter the Kingdom of God (John 3:3, 5), while the unregenerate, unsaved, unbeliever (one who has not been born again) will not enter into the Kingdom of God but will instead face eternal judgment (Revelation 20:11–15).

The "new creation" of a born again person has been taken from death in trespasses and sins and made alive (Ephesians 2:1).

A born again person has been baptized by the Holy Spirit into the body of Christ (1 Corinthians 12:13).

A born again person has been sealed by the Holy Spirit until the day of redemption (Ephesians 1:13, 4:30). And the gift of the Holy Spirit is merely the *earnest* or down-payment of an inheritance for the born again person that is unchanging, pure and unfailing (1 Peter 1:4).

So you see, there are many real, tangible and substantial changes that are involved in being a new creation. These are not things that occur merely as a consequence of sitting in church, or making up one's mind to be different or becoming "religious." Christianity is not a religion, IT IS CHRIST!

To truly grasp the idea of a born again "new creation," you must look at the difference between a caterpillar and a butterfly.

The caterpillar is fuzzy, has a long body with many legs, built to be earthbound and has no

> There are many substantial changes that are involved in being a new creation.

hope of flight. But it reaches a point when it is ready to be "born again," and is secluded and separated from the other caterpillars and is wrapped in the mysterious world of a cocoon.

A transformation happens in the cocoon and the caterpillar is changed inside and out. When it emerges, it is no longer a caterpillar at all, but is now a butterfly. This new creature is different in every way: it is sleek and aerodynamic; it has beautiful wings and is specifically designed for flight.

This new creature, this butterfly is certainly not a caterpillar that has "gotten religion" and it is not a caterpillar that has decided to turn its life around and it is not a caterpillar that has merely decided that the time has come to live a butterfly lifestyle! This butterfly is a former caterpillar that is now an entirely NEW CREATURE!

This physical transformation I have described mirrors the

spiritual transformation described by the prophet Ezekiel as he relayed what God told him to tell the nation of Israel about the new birth that would be made possible by the New Covenant.

> For I will take you from among the nations, gather you out of all countries, and bring you into your own land. Then I will sprinkle clean water on you, and you shall be clean; I will cleanse you from all your filthiness and from all your idols. I will give you a new heart and put a new spirit within you; I will take the heart of stone out of your flesh and give you a heart of flesh. I will put My Spirit within you and cause you to walk in My statutes, and you will keep My judgments and do *them* (Ezekiel 36:24–27).

Just like the caterpillar, God takes the person in his natural state. He has a body, mind and soul that are definitely "earthbound." In our natural state, we love the lusts of the flesh and to satisfy every sinful and carnal desire of the flesh.

We love to smoke, drink, intoxicate ourselves, fornicate and disobey God with every form of infidelity, adultery, deceit and covetous greed. We entertain ourselves with movies, music and TV shows heavily themed with murder, prostitution, homosexuality, illicit sexual activity and violence. We are unforgiving, selfish, obsessive and impatient.

But one day, we reach a point when we have the desire

to be "born again." We realize that the way we've been living is really not "living" at all, but a walking death in our sins and trespasses.

Ezekiel describes how God takes us away and separates us from the other "caterpillars" and sprinkles the clean water of His life-giving Word to cleanse our thinking and turn us away from false gods and filthy living.

> The way we've been living is really not "living" at all, but a walking death.

He performs heart surgery upon us and removes the old wicked desires and feelings and replaces them with a new heart that loves Him and desires to serve Him. With the new Spirit of God within us, we now desire to walk in His statutes and follow His commandments.

We emerge from the "cocoon" of His care by and through the faith that Christ is Savior and Lord, and that He was crucified for our sins and raised from the dead, and that by His sacrifice, we are justified (considered righteous) before God.

And as we emerge, we are born again! We are new creatures! We are new creations of God with new hearts, new spirits, new desires, and new positions with God as temples of His Holy Spirit who are sealed to receive an eternal inheritance from Him! Hallelujah!

Friends, right now, place your faith where God judged your sins: at the cross of Christ! *If you can and will confess openly, unashamedly and truthfully right now that Jesus is your Lord and **you believe in your heart** that God has raised Him from* *the dead because He has paid your penalty for sin in full, then you will be saved* (Romans 10:9–10, 4:23–35)!

The heart in which you believe unto salvation is the new heart Ezekiel promised you as a basic element of the new covenant of the new birth! Glory! If you have received the new heart *now* you've been born again!

But even as a butterfly, you still also have your old caterpillar memories, desires and tendencies to overcome. You must learn how to fly and experience the joy of soaring as the new creature God has made you rather than returning to your old caterpillar ways.

You now have victory over sin and death, over lusts and desires of the flesh, over habits, addictions and strongholds! You are no longer a slave to sin, but rather one who can soar above it on godly wings made specifically for your new birth!

Only the Beginning

I believe the greatest flaw in American evangelism today, aside from there not being enough of it going on, is that it is used as a means to an end. The salvation of God in the blood of the

Lord Jesus Christ is not an *end;* it is the *beginning* of an eternal relationship.

The Bible tells us that we are *adopted* by the Father in the blood of Christ. Imagine a prospective father going to an orphanage, falling in love with a child and deciding to make the child his heir. Then after going through all the paperwork, all the procedures, and all the expense to see the work of adoption finished, he signs the papers, seals the adoption, pats the child on the head and walks away saying, "Well, that's it! We're finished. Have a nice life. I'll see you in Heaven."

That would be crazy! A parent's adoption of a child is only the beginning of a new life together. It's only after the *procedure* of the adoption is complete that the *purpose* of the adoption can be fulfilled.

Do you really think that all your Heavenly Father intends to have from His relationship with you purchased by the shedding of the precious blood of Christ is to see you at church once or twice a week? Do you really? If so, then you devalue the preciousness of the blood *and* the Lamb, so much so, that I would even question whether your grasp of the gospel is firm enough to have laid a hold of your Savior at all.

God paid the incalculable price of shedding the blood of the Lamb so that He could robe you in His righteousness, fill you with His Spirit, and bless you with healing, health, liberty and abundance in every realm of life: spiritual, emotional, psychological, physical, financial and material.

By His blood, we have escaped from the certainty of hell

that awaits the unregenerate, unbelievers who will die in their unrepentant rejection of Christ. But if *hell* is what we have *escaped from,* we have to ask ourselves what have we *been born into?*

The Bible tells us that we have been translated **out** of darkness and **into** the Kingdom of His dear Son.

I hear people say all the time that if the Lord didn't do a thing for them after He saved them, He has already done enough. I guess they think that sounds humble and grateful and holy.

First of all, if the Lord didn't do anything for you after He saved you, then He'd be a liar according to all the promises He's pledged toward you in His Word. But even if you don't read your Bible enough to know what God has promised you because of the preciousness and value of the blood with which He paid for you, common sense should tell you He's better than the kind of derelict father we'd prosecute as a criminal.

What father would we allow to escape the consequences of our justice system who laid claim on a child and then never gave that child any protection or provision, never fed or clothed him, sheltered or protected him, educated or encouraged him, or taught him how to live, learn and take dominion and authority over the family's property? What would we do with a father who, after he claimed the child, never did anything else? We'd denounce him for certain and arrest him if possible, that's what!

And I can tell you for a certainty that after the Lord saved me, if He hadn't done anything else for me, I would still be a mess!

The Rest of the Story

The Sunday after our baptisms, Nicky Simmons became Nicky Turner and I became the happiest and most blessed man on earth. We were saved, baptized, newly married, crazy in love and free from the ravages of my addictions and able to look forward to our future.

But when we took a good look at our future, we realized there wasn't a whole lot to shout about in what we could see on the horizon. Knowing that we were assured of Heaven was worthy of our joy, but the debt, lack and uncertainty of the here and now, clouded the anticipation of the hereafter.

I'd been raised from death, but I needed to build a life. Hosting call-in shows at the radio station was a part-time job and I needed a full-time career.

I'd lost virtually everything I owned, my credit was destroyed, I owed the Internal Revenue Service tens of thousands of dollars, and my name and reputation were still in the mud.

It was primarily the all too recent destruction of my reputation that made me laugh out loud when my former agent suggested the possibility of returning to television news in Detroit. But I agreed to let him put out some discreet "feelers" on one condition: that under no circumstances would he call Channel 7 to mention my name.

I remember telling him that I knew for a certainty, that was the one place in the entire world where I would *never* be able to work again, and I didn't even want the embarrassment of anyone there laughing at me over an inquiry.

But not only was I soon going to return to the anchor chair, it was indeed to be the chair I declared impossible for me to have. And I wouldn't just be returning to deliver the usual *bad* news.

God had a plan for me to return to the very same anchor chair from which my personal and professional demise had been reported. He planned for me to claim victory as a trophy of His grace and a witness to declare the good news of salvation in the Kingdom of God by faith in the shed blood of Jesus Christ; and to be the first to do it regularly as part of a major market, network affiliated, secular newscast.

> Not only was I to return to the anchor chair, it was the chair I declared impossible for me to have.

CHAPTER TEN

AMERICA'S FIRST EVANGELICAL ANCHORMAN

"Now when they bring you to the synagogues and
magistrates and authorities, do not worry about
how or what you should answer, or what
you should say. For the Holy Spirit
will teach you in that very hour
what you ought to say"
(Luke 12:11–12).

The day after Nicky and I were married, her aunt Alyce was diagnosed with lung cancer. In November of that same year, she died. If she had lived just five months longer, she would have seen the realization of something only she believed was possible.

Actually, Alyce never once said she *thought* I *might* return to Channel 7, she always declared that she knew I would as a *certainty*. Whenever Alyce would announce that she *knew* I would return to the anchor desk, my wife and I would always smile politely and then one of us would give the other *that look* behind her back.

You know, *that look* where you kind of half roll your eyes and raise your eyebrows in that universal sign that somebody just said something crazy.

Sometimes when she said it, I would attempt to straighten her out, to educate her in the finer points of television protocol, destroyed opportunities and flat out impossibilities concerning things that obviously she didn't understand. "You just don't know how these things work," I would tell her. She never wavered in her prediction.

When I did actually return to Channel 7 on April 17, 2000 as a reporter and weekend co-anchor, it was nothing short of a miracle and it made headlines. I made sure that all the headlines reported it as the miracle it was by my bold declaration that it was the Lord Jesus Christ who was singularly responsible.

> When I did return to Channel 7, it was a miracle and it made headlines.

Had I not been saved, delivered from addiction, and physically and emotionally healed by the Lord Jesus Christ, I would never have even lived to see April of 2000, let alone celebrate it.

Even among those who stepped up to claim that they had a hand in my return—that it was either their influence or an idea that they initiated which led to me being re-hired—none could claim that it was their hand that reached into my chest and restored my lungs, healed my heart, or laid hold on my addictions and snatched them from me.

No one could say that it was their influence with God and not the blood of Christ that moved Him to extend to me the grace of my salvation.

The credit belonged solely to Christ and I boldly gave witness to His mercy, His grace and His name in every interview, inquiry, article, and broadcast.

Looking back at exactly *how* this miraculous resurrection of my career unfolded, it is easy to see that the Lord Himself orchestrated every move.

The Talk of the Town

I was a born evangelist from the moment I was born again. And as Peter was sent to be the Apostle to the Jews and Paul to be the Apostle to the Gentiles, I guess you might say that I was sent to be the apostle to the secular media.

The miracles by which the Lord orchestrated my return to the anchor chair at Channel 7 are truly astounding. After I was raised from the dead, He used my boldness in boasting of my healing and restoration during my radio call-in programs to spread the word of my miraculous change and deliverance from drug addiction.

With such a buzz about town that *Frank Turner is different, Frank Turner has been born again, Frank Turner has completely lost his mind and is babbling all the time about Jesus*, all kinds of opportunities to share my testimony suddenly sprang up including the one that eventually led to my return to the station.

There was an idea at Channel 7 that perhaps an interesting November ratings period piece about what I was doing with my life after television might interest viewers. After all that had happened in the time since I had been fired, I was anxious to set the record straight, and to let viewers see the new me.

I confessed my former addictions, explained my brief comedy career, corrected and refuted all the false statements and wild rumors surrounding me and boldly gave a testimony of my miraculous salvation and immediate deliverance from addiction and death by the Lord Jesus Christ.

The response from viewers who called, e-mailed and wrote letters by the thousands was overwhelming to the station and me.

And that paved the way for another idea: that perhaps putting Frank Turner back on television might be a good move. One thing led to another. There were meetings, discussions and more meetings.

There were questions. What happens if he ends up back on drugs? What happens if we put him on and he's unstable? What if more people hate him than like him? What difference does it make if they'll still watch?

From me, there was only one answer. I met with the upper levels of the station management, and I gave them my testimony. Not as detailed as I'm sharing with you now, but enough that I believe the Holy Spirit melted their hearts with it and opened the door that had been locked behind me when I was thrown out.

> I met with the upper levels of the station management, and I gave them my testimony.

What no one knew at the time was that the job I was being given back wasn't really the resurrection of a television news career, but the platform for the launching of an international ministry of evangelism.

The greatest miracle of all was that God was orchestrating my opportunity to become the first news anchor in the history of television to regularly proclaim the gospel of salvation by faith in the Lord Jesus Christ in nightly commentaries, from the news desk of a major market, network affiliated, secular newscast.

Christians in the Closet

There are a lot of people who call themselves Christians in the secular media and some of them are even actually saved born again believers. But most of them you couldn't find with a spotlight. And a lot of the people you'd assume are believers because of the *religious phrases* they like to sling around are nothing but cheap imitations.

> The woodwork of the secular media is bursting with closet Christians who refuse to come out.

As with most secular industries, the woodwork of the secular media is bursting with closet Christians who refuse to come out. There are untold numbers of "Secret Service" saints working undercover and born again believers who are hiding out like they're in some kind of Jehovah's Witness Protection Program.

It gets back to the whole *religion* thing. People who are either just pretending or practicing Christianity falsely as a *mere form of godliness* that denies the true power of the gospel for salvation, are able to timidly compartmentalize their faith. They can fit it into a neat little box where they can keep a lid on it and make sure they don't get any on you.

Authentic, growing, mature, blood-covered, blood-bought, born again, Spirit-filled, children of the Most High God live in recognition that they have been snatched from the jaws of death, hell, and the grave. Having been translated into the Kingdom of God's Dear Son, they *are not timid people when it comes to standing up for the gospel of their salvation!*

The very same people, who will rush to their feet to raise an argument about how the secular media is an inappropriate outlet for the discussion of Christ as *Savior*, have no trouble discussing Christ when portrayed as a liar, womanizer, charlatan or as a figment of the imaginations of religious fanatics.

The same media people who claim to be so careful as not to "offend" anyone with the doctrine of salvation, have no trouble offending people with the abominations of pornography, homosexuality, adultery, abortion, blasphemy, profanity and nudity.

> Saved or unsaved, I have never been hemmed in by the boundaries of political correctness.

Saved or unsaved, I have never been hemmed in by the boundaries of political correctness. Before and after salvation, I have always expressed exactly what was in my heart.

In Matthew 12:34 and Luke 6:45 the Lord says that out of the abundance of the heart, the mouth speaks. In other words, whatever is in your heart is going to come out of your mouth.

People who claim to have the Lord Jesus in their hearts, but only excuses for not saying His name on their lips, have their hearts filled with denial instead of deliverance.

Before I was re-hired by Channel 7, I had demonstrated my irrepressible boldness for proclaiming my testimony of healing and deliverance and the gospel of my salvation.

The last days of my part-time fill-ins on the radio as a call-in show host were particularly irritating for the management. Day after day, I was admonished to stop talking about *religion* on the air. I actually never talked about religion; I always talked about the Lord Jesus Christ, but I knew what they meant.

After my baptism, I looked different, sounded different, acted differently and people who called the show wanted to know why, so I told them about Jesus and how He had dramatically changed my life and healed my body.

My thoughts and perspectives were different, my opinions changed, and my priorities were realigned. Callers wanted to know how and why my perspectives had shifted so dramatically and so quickly. So, I told them I was studying the Bible.

Then people, some of whom had never actually opened a Bible, started calling in to the program to argue about Scriptures with me. So, I opened my Bible and started trying to set them straight.

All of this continually brought managers into my booth to tell me, "This isn't a Christian radio station!" and "Put that Bible down and talk about stuff that's in the newspaper!"

But my heart was so filled with the Lord that I couldn't discuss any aspect of any topic without in some way relating it back to God and His Word.

Not to mention the fact that just months earlier, I was a helpless, hopeless drug addict with a bad heart and a destroyed life! All of a sudden, I had a wife, I had a life, and I even suddenly had a ministry sharing the gospel with addicts in drug treatment; how was I not going to talk about my whole life being raised from the dead by Jesus?

> How was I not going to talk about my whole life being raised from the dead by Jesus?

It is amazing that anyone, anytime, anywhere can publicly espouse any kind of viewpoint or opinion and while it may be considered arguable, it is still considered viable unless its origin is Biblical.

Discussions of a "mere mortal" Jesus are acceptable as long as the discussion is about "following" Him or "denouncing" Him, but when the discussion is about the "Lord" Jesus and being "saved" by Him and attaining Heaven by faith in the forgiveness of sin because of His shed blood and empty tomb; suddenly you have done the unforgivable and you may even be condemned as a fool.

But here's the thing:

For since, in the wisdom of God, the world through wisdom did not know God, it pleased God through the foolishness of the message preached to save those who believe (1 Corinthians 1:21).

God uses the *foolishness* of preaching to save the lost. No one can believe the gospel until someone is "foolishly" willing to risk everything for the opportunity to tell them.

I didn't specifically intend to use Channel 7 as a platform to preach the gospel, but from the moment I was saved, delivered, and healed, I planned to use *every* opportunity as a platform to preach the gospel whether or not I happened to be in a place where it was considered acceptable.

The principles of duty, honor and responsibility extend far beyond the limitations of *arbitrary* protocols and opinions. Banging on the door of someone's cabin

> I planned to use every opportunity as a platform to preach the gospel.

aboard a ship in the middle of the night is inappropriate, unless it is to warn them that *the ship is sinking*.

Kicking in someone's door at 3:00 in the morning and snatching someone out of bed to carry him outside is breaking and entering and kidnapping, unless *his house is ablaze*.

If true Christianity were merely a "belief system," if the truth of Christ was only an "opinion," if being born again was only a *religious pursuit* instead of a tangible, actual, verifiable reality, then it would be nothing short of inappropriate *not* to confine the gospel within the walls of church buildings, and to never make mention of it in the public square.

But the fact that *this world is a sinking ship* whose passengers are doomed; the fact that *it is a house ablaze* whose occupants are condemned to a fiery death makes it *a crime against man and a sin before God not to proclaim the salvation through the blood of His Christ to the expense of everything else*!

It is wrong for a person to grab a child they don't know, unless for instance, they have dived into a lake to rescue the child from drowning.

It is wrong for a man to grab and tightly embrace a woman on the street who is a complete stranger to him, unless for instance, it is to pull her out of the path of an oncoming vehicle.

Our actions in evangelizing the lost through the unhindered sharing of the gospel must be judged by the reality of the consequences for *refusing* to act, rather than the ridicule or scorn we may face for *choosing* to act.

Consider this:

"For God did not send His Son into the world to condemn the world, but that the world through Him might be saved. He who believes in Him is not condemned; but he who does not believe is condemned already, because he has not believed in the name of the only begotten Son of God" (John 3:17–18).

For two thousand years, the weight and gravity of the Lord's Words here have been continually and foolishly disregarded.

Jesus is telling us plainly how the severity of our situation requires the necessity of His blood sacrifice.

Judgment is not a mere *possibility* that is *potentially* looming over the heads of *some* of the people of this world; it is the *certain* reality of *everyone who rejects the salvation made possible only by His sacrifice.*

Eternal torment is the future to which mankind *has already been condemned* for his evil nature, evidenced by the world he has shaped and the way he behaves in it. God is not sending people to hell, but rather, He is giving them a way out by offering His Son as our substitution.

> Preaching the gospel to the lost is the requirement of securing their rescue.

This means by rejecting the Son of God, you are rejecting the only escape from the inevitable consequences of living in the sin from which Christ died to free you.

Preaching the gospel to the lost, therefore, is not the option of practicing a religion; it is the requirement of securing their rescue.

If as the Lord said, out of the abundance of the heart the mouth speaks, then speaking from the news desk about salvation by faith in the name of Jesus was simply a matter of speaking from the heart.

The Foolishness of Preaching

> For the preaching of the cross is to them that perish
> foolishness; but unto us which are saved it is the
> power of God (1 Corinthians 1:18).

Preaching the gospel is foolishness. God declares it, the Word of God confirms it, and there is no denying it. Preaching the Cross is foolishness.

The Scripture makes it clear that not only is the preaching of the Cross foolishness but that the foolishness is not a matter of *where* you are preaching the gospel, but *to whom* you are preaching it.

Preaching the gospel *to **them that perish*** is foolishness, but *to **us which are saved*** it is the power of God.

So, the matter of whether some *places* are more or less appropriate for preaching is actually the wrong premise. The difference between the message being foolish or being powerful is not *where* it is being spoken but to *whom*; whether the people hearing it are rejecting the Cross to remain lost (foolishness) or believing in the Cross to be saved (powerful) is the true distinction.

Therefore, the preaching of the Cross by a television anchor during a news broadcast on Monday night is no more foolish than the preaching of the Cross by a pastor in a church pulpit on Sunday morning. It is not about the *location of the preaching*, but rather the *reaction to the preaching*.

That realization caused me to make an important decision concerning my approach to evangelism and the preaching of the Cross, and I believe based on my decision, God made His decision concerning my future.

In essence, I decided that I would broadcast the gospel; that I would make it my mission to preach the gospel to *everyone* rather than preaching it *everywhere*. And He decided to give me the platform to do it.

Here is the distinction. The gospel is not to be preached *in places*, but rather it is to be preached *to people*. If you read the history of the birth of the Church in the book of The Acts of the Apostles (the first book after the four gospels), you'll see that the Apostles did not wait for people who wanted the *power of salvation* to come to them. They went out and preached the gospel *as foolishness to the lost people who would perish without it*.

They turned foolishness into power by preaching the lost into their salvation.

The Apostles went to temples of idolatry and temples of Judaism; they went to shrines where people worshipped false gods and to seats of government where legislators and philosophers passed laws and debated worldly wisdom.

They were just as likely to be refused, rejected, jailed, and even beaten when they preached at the temples, where the discussion of God *should have been considered the most appropriate and most welcome*, as they were when they preached at the councils or in marketplaces.

Some people rejected the message as foolishness and

others accepted it as the power of their salvation. It never made any difference whether the *place* in which the message was delivered was deemed *appropriate*.

Likewise, I determined that since the preaching of the Cross was considered foolishness no matter where it was preached, until it converted the hearts of the hearers and became the power of salvation, I would have *no personal restrictions about where I would proclaim Christ. If there were lost people listening who could be saved, who could hear the foolishness and receive power, then that would be my only criterion.*

> I would have *no personal restrictions about where I would proclaim Christ.*

Whether there was opposition, rejection, persecution or ridicule; regardless of the location, medium, protocol or prior practice; I would always be willing to "broadcast" the gospel to the ears of whoever might hear, no matter who else thought I was being foolish.

By the time I returned to television, my resolve for spreading the gospel had already birthed my ministry as a traveling evangelist. The word of my awesome and powerful testimony was spreading rapidly and I was a regular guest on Christian radio and television shows.

I was also preaching and witnessing everywhere I was invited, from churches to the living and dining rooms of residential drug treatment houses.

To the interviewers covering my return to Channel 7, I

preached Christ; in the articles quoting me about my return, I preached Christ. To every possible inquiry and question concerning my return, the answer was Christ.

I presented the Cross on television, on the radio, in the newsroom, at the grocery store, in the mall, and even on the street corner.

As I talked about the Lord openly during the newscasts at every opportunity, the consensus among many of my friends and acquaintances was that I was going to get fired (and that I had lost my mind). But instead, the Lord kept increasing my territory.

> The more I have been willing to preach without permission, the more God has granted permission for me to preach.

I was promoted from weekend anchor to the 5:00 weekday evening newscast. More media buzz, more proclamation of Christ. More fear from friends that I would get fired.

I was promoted to anchor an additional evening newscast at 7:00 weeknights. More media buzz, more proclamation of Christ. More fear from friends.

Then, knowing what I would say given any opportunity, one day my boss announced he would give me a segment at the end of the 7:00 newscast *to say whatever I wanted in a nightly commentary. What?!*

I hear people moaning and groaning about all the restrictions and opposition to the preaching of Christ in America, but that has not been my experience at all. *The more I have been willing to preach without permission, the more God has granted permission for me to preach.*

Finally Tonight...Making History

"Finally tonight...." It became my sign off and my signal. It told viewers that the newscast was over and a personal word from its anchor was about to begin. It signaled that the closing thought to end the newscast, tie a ribbon on my broadcast day and express with my mouth the abundance of my heart was coming next.

Each night to end the 7:00 news broadcast, I spoke candidly, clearly, pointedly and without restriction. Our agreement allowed me to have the freedom to say whatever was on my heart, even if that also included talking about Jesus.

The key was authenticity. My commentary could be humorous or serious, it could be political or social, it could challenge or chasten, and I was allowed to confer criticism or pronounce praise. But the key was authenticity. My words had to be genuine and heartfelt and so my topics had to be without restriction.

It wasn't church *every* night. But on many nights, it was. And I warned viewers in advance about what would be coming:

Frank's Final Thoughts

Finally tonight: "Frank's Final Thoughts" and why I take the opportunity of this little segment to say the things I do.

First of all, I don't like to mince words. The airwaves are already filled with so much empty and ridiculous rhetoric, political pandering, shameful behavior and shameless self-promotion that it's time somebody just "told it like it is."

I like to focus on social ills and the people and agencies most responsible for perpetuating them. Those are the ones I hope will make you mad enough to call someone up, vote someone out or shout someone down.

I like to stir up patriotism for the country and criticism for the people running and shaping it. America is beautiful and its ideals noble, but let's face it—taxes are too high, our money completely mismanaged, and government is totally out of touch. Most social activism has been reduced to rabble-rousing. And instead of real action, you get blowhards using platitudes to stir up trouble.

I bash prime-time sleaze TV a lot. If you like it, don't take that personally. But I'm not kidding around—I really think its bad for our children and us.

And speaking of children—remember, the generation we're hurting will hurt us back.

And often, I speak of the Lord Jesus Christ. That upsets some people when I'm on TV. They should see me when I'm off; He's all I talk about.

Frank Turner

Over the nearly two year span of my commentary segment, I challenged government to be better and chastened politicians for putting their interests above the people they were elected to serve.

I criticized waste and mismanagement in public school administration, I disputed the motives of most so-called social activists, and I attacked the ABC network of which Channel 7 is an affiliate, for its lewd and shameful offerings of prime-time adultery, drug use, homosexuality and fornication.

I waged war on everything from the liberal deterioration of moral values in America to the occasional idiotic declaration of a "Dixie Chick."

I often spoke on behalf of people with no platform, championed the causes of consumers with no recourse, and I defended the downtrodden while encouraging our heroes.

All of my opinions, all of my perspectives, all of my positions were Biblical in origin, godly in intention and authentic in presentation.

But the commentaries that caused me to be beamed around the world on satellite broadcasts from the sets of *Life Today with James and Betty Robison*, *Praise the Lord!* on the Trinity Broadcasting Network, *The 700 Club*, *TCT Alive* on the Total Christian Television Network and many others, were the historic proclamations never before made by an anchorman on a secular nightly newscast.

History was made with the words "Finally tonight..." when they were followed by messages like this one celebrating my daughter Ally's first birthday:

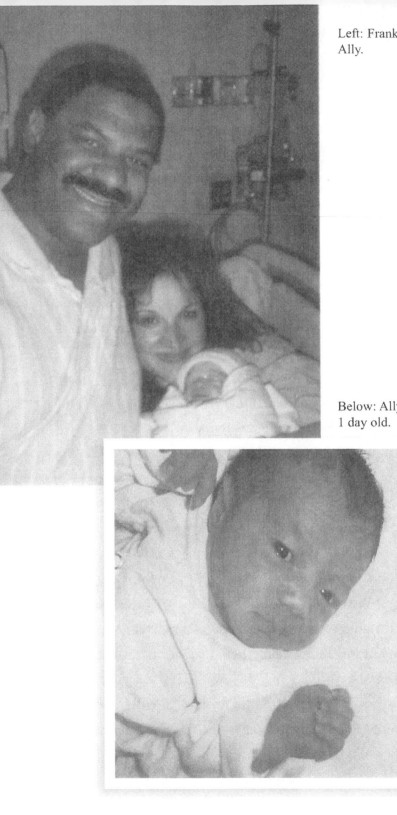

Left: Frank, Nicky and newborn Ally.

Below: Allyson Patton Turner, 1 day old.

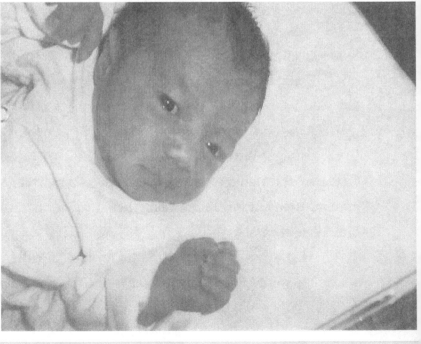

Fatherhood

Finally tonight: fatherhood and why my first year of it has been the best year of my life.

Every child is a gift from God; every birth is a miracle. But the birth of my child, my little Allyson Patton Turner, is the pinnacle of so many miracles in my life that began after I was born again.

One year ago today, my wife Nicky brought Allyson into the world and our wildest dream into reality. We've called her Ally, *Pooh Bear, Hookus Pookus Mcgookus* and for several weeks in the beginning, *Screaming Night Terror*.

Never before had I understood love on this level: unconditional, overwhelming, all-consuming and so deep it feels as if my heart might sometimes explode with joy.

She is the light in my life, the reason to awaken, the purpose for living.

Living, for me, is a miracle in itself. Four years ago, my life was a walking death of hopeless addictions that had destroyed my mind, my body and my soul. But in accepting that Christ died for me, I was reborn to live for Him and Nicky and Ally.

Four years ago this month, I gave my life to Christ. One year ago today, He gave Allyson's life to me. I'm sure I got the better of both deals.

These commentaries represent the most startling and single most significant development in American evangelism since the invention of television. There are twenty-four hour *Christian* television networks that provide Christian programming and the constant presentation of the gospel message.

But only one man in the history of the medium has commandeered secular airwaves for Christ in the way that I did.

I did it in response to the awesome deliverance I received. I responded to God and God responded to me. This was a sovereign and miraculous move of God Himself. I was only chosen to be His instrument in a season that He had predetermined was going to come. But because I responded with boldness and without hesitation, I have reaped the reward of being unique among all the world's evangelists for this historic accomplishment.

James Robison invited me to be on *Life Today* when he saw this one:

The National Day of Prayer

Finally tonight: the National Day of Prayer and why an entire nation focused today on talking to God might be better off listening.

A nation listening to God might have less profanity and nudity in its prime time television programs. It might reduce the average of ten thousand acts of television violence watched annually by each of its children. It might remove the rape scenes filmed for one of every eight Hollywood movies. It might cancel *The Bachelor.*

A nation listening to God might not consume billions in drugs, pornography and alcohol while throwing billions more away at casinos, racetracks and lottery machines.

A nation listening to God might care for its elderly, feed its poor and protect its children.

The Bible promises that God rewards those that diligently seek Him. This nation should try it while closing our mouths and opening our ears.

Frank Turner

Here's my personal favorite. Before you cast a vote for a so-called "Christian" running for office, make sure they meet the standards of the next commentary:

The Government and the Church

Finally tonight: the Government and the Church and why Christian candidates who claim to have Christ in their heart but not in their politics are either liars or fools.

There is a raging debate over whether Christian politicians should leave Christ at the door when they step into office.

The constitutional separation of Church and State is arguable, but the Bible is explicitly clear that the Christian cannot be separated from Christ.

Followers of Christ are to use their lives to reflect His character, their speech to proclaim His gospel and present their bodies as a living sacrifice to Him.

Christians are called to filter their thoughts through the mind of Christ and not only to believe, but to act on that belief; to be doers of the Word of God and not just hearers.

Whether this is proper for a politician may be arguable, but it is required of every Christian whether they enter politics or not.

Christian candidates who claim Christ has no place in their politics are either lying about what they believe or foolish enough to abandon it for political gain.

And from either liar or fool, you'll never get good
government.

Frank Turner

Every American holiday provides an opportunity to preach the Cross, especially Independence Day:

The Fourth of July

Finally tonight: the Fourth of July and why the celebration of freedom in America is a good time to at least consider the possibility of freedom for eternity.

This freedom we enjoy was purchased at a great price. The founders of this nation forged a contract with liberty that many have signed in their blood. The slaves who were brought here in chains were beaten to bear its burdens on their backs. The pioneers who settled it sacrificed themselves to blaze a trail we could follow.

But this liberty has its limitations. We are still bound by our hatreds and prejudices, our weaknesses and addictions, our lusts and desires, and as sure as we live, we will die.

The Gospel tells us there is another contract with liberty signed in the blood of Jesus Christ—He alone has borne the burden of our sin and He has blazed a trail into eternity that we can follow. His promise is that whosoever lives and believes in Him shall never die.

If freedom in America is worth celebrating, isn't the possibility of freedom for eternity at least worth considering?

Frank Turner

Among my favorite topics to tackle was prayer. Often, I tried to challenge the thinking of believers to move out of the *religious* nonsense being taught about prayer and into the reality that prayer cannot be restricted or hindered by government; only abandoned by believers:

Prayer in Public Schools

Finally tonight: prayer in public schools and why it's time we settle the question of why the Christian Political Right has been so wrong on this issue.

That Christians cannot pray in and for our public school system is a fallacy fostered by people whose agenda is more political than prayerful.

These are people who prefer the spectacle of fighting for the right for their prayers to be seen and heard by other people, rather than offered to and answered by God.

The responsibility for the lack of prayer in school lies not in the ruling of the court, but squarely at the feet of those commanded by Christ to pray, regardless of whether a court gives them permission.

Prayer is not a right to be granted or rescinded by a legal ruling of the Supreme Court, but a responsibility and privilege given as a gift from the Supreme Being.

Any Christian, anywhere and at any time, can pray without hindrance and should without hesitation. And prohibitions against praying are impossible to enforce on those occasions when, as the Lord suggests, only you and He know you're doing it.

Prayer is allowed in public schools and every other institution when offered as a private petition and not a public performance.

Frank Turner

I need to add a note concerning Easter Weekend. I could not ignore it as an opportunity to preach the Cross of Christ and His empty tomb. But in a minute long commentary segment, I also could not correct nearly 2000 years of errant tradition ingrained in the Church largely through Roman Catholicism.

Modern church tradition cannot reconcile that Christ was crucified on a Friday, raised on a Sunday and yet fulfilled Scripture by spending three days and nights in the grave.

I have heard some pretty far-fetched explanations trying to turn myth into math, but it just doesn't add up. In spite of the "Good Friday" tradition, you can't squeeze three days and three nights into the period between Friday afternoon and Sunday morning no matter how you try. The Lord was crucified on a Wednesday.

But in this instance, I chose to use the established tradition to make a larger point, rather than try to correct bad theology. Therefore, I am using "Good Friday" in the next commentary as a time-honored tradition rather than a Biblical reality.

Good Friday

Finally tonight: Good Friday and why it was the badness of the last bad Thursday that made the first Good Friday really good.

The value of the Good News in the Gospel of the Lord Jesus Christ wouldn't be as good if not for the price of the bad news that His atonement paid.

For instance, the wages of sin is death. On Thursday, you had to pay your own way. On Good Friday, Christ paid for everyone who would believe.

On Thursday, a thief was fearing death on the cross with no hope of Heaven. On Good Friday, that same thief was hoping for Heaven with no fear of death.

On Thursday, the Cross was a painful place on which to die. On Good Friday, the Cross became the promise of grace in which to rest.

For millions of Christians, it is all that was bad on that last bad Thursday that allows us to appreciate what was really good about that first Good Friday.

Frank Turner

The Resurrection of Jesus

Finally tonight: the resurrection of Jesus Christ and why the empty tomb is really the centerpiece of this holiday weekend.

It is a mistake to believe that there would not be an Easter without the Resurrection. At its origin, Easter had much more to do with a celebration of fertility and renewal than with Christ, which explains the association with rabbits and eggs.

There are also special traditions of family celebrations, particularly for children; thus the chocolate, candy, Easter outfits and bonnets.

But on that first Sunday after Christ had been crucified, there was a celebration that had nothing to do with bunnies or bonnets. The tomb in which the crucified Christ had been laid was empty because the resurrected Christ had risen.

And for 2000 years, rather than "a" resurrection, it is still called "the" Resurrection, securing the singular place of the Lord Jesus Christ in history and that empty tomb as the real centerpiece of this holiday weekend.

Frank Turner

Night after night, week after week, I historically and uniquely presented powerful Christian themes, teaching and even preaching in a one-minute presentation at the end of a secular newscast:

The Promises Fulfilled

Finally tonight: the promises fulfilled and why we miss the Christians who are taken from us, but they wouldn't want to come back.

The Lord Jesus Christ tells believers in Him that though they may die, yet shall they live. To the unbeliever, it is a paradox; but to the believer, it is a promise.

The promise is an assurance that His perfect life provides the gift of righteousness through grace, that His atoning death is the perfect sacrifice to pay for sin and that His resurrection is the perfect victory over death and the grave.

The promise of Christ removes fear and erases doubt; it turns the unknown into the certain and replaces anxiety over death with the peaceful anticipation of paradise.

It is impossible to lay aside our longing for those we have lost. No matter the circumstances, we often miss most those whose company we can no longer enjoy. We selfishly want them with us as we continue in this world.

But absent from their bodies, the Bible promises that believers are present with the Lord. And in His presence, His promises are fulfilled.

Frank Turner

Sin

Finally tonight: sin and why what the Bible says about sin should separate the thinking of Bible believers from everyone else.

In this new age, it seems that sin has replaced all previous four-lettered forms of profanity to become the world's only dirty word.

The same people who consider God's commandments simply *suggestions* and His pronouncements merely *platitudes*, are now successfully promoting that His prohibitions are to be disregarded as outdated expressions of intolerance, and engaging in those prohibited behaviors is never to be regarded as sin.

In fact, the only sin that today's tolerance will not indulge is calling it sin. Instead, people use words like *choice, alternative, lifestyle* and *personal freedom*.

And that is why this tiny word with huge implications should separate Bible believers from everyone else. While we don't have to argue it, defend it, fight over it or debate it, we most definitely should never stop using it.

Frank Turner

Leftovers

Finally tonight: leftovers and why, in many ways, a meal and a message are actually better the second day.

Millions of Christians went home from church Sunday, ideally after having their spirits fed by a hearty message, to sit down and have their bodies fed by a hearty meal. If both the message and the meal were truly good, then hopefully there was too much of both for either to be consumed in one sitting.

A lot of meals just get better when you warm them up again... the meat is more flavorful...the spices and seasonings in the sauces and gravies have had a chance to set in and mingle. The memory of how good it was, combined with the anticipation of how good it will be, wakes up the taste buds to experience something they missed the day before.

For Christians, that Sunday message about the Lord Jesus Christ should also be even better warmed up in the heart on the day after. The "meat" of the message should be more flavorful in your mind. The implications of the impact of His life upon yours have had a chance to set in and mingle with your thoughts. And in the memory of the message, you might even experience something you missed the day before.

Of course, meals and messages left too long get stale. You need to have seconds while they're still fresh.

Frank Turner

The Gospel Truth

Finally Tonight: The Gospel Truth and why it seems people are willing to look just about everywhere for it, except where they are certain to find it.

"The Da Vinci Code" is merely the latest in a series of slanderous salvos aimed at dragging the man, the message and the mission of Jesus Christ through the mud.

It amazes me that so many people are combing the pages of this ridiculous book hoping to discover a new truth about the Lord.

For two thousand years, the truth about Christ has been available from the lips of apostles who traveled with Him, from hundreds of disciples who witnessed His works, and from the gospels, written down to provide a permanent record of His sinless life, atoning death and eternal resurrection.

And yet, books that belittle Him, Broadway scores that reduce Him to misguided "Superstar" status and movies that weave lies of His womanizing, continue to thrive on popular demand.

There is obviously, a vast audience searching for something to believe about Jesus. But if you're looking for the Gospel Truth, the Gospels should be the first place you look.

Frank Turner

The Sin of Adultery

Finally tonight: marriage and why it's a shame the sin of adultery isn't considered more of a crime.

Adultery does to marriage what head-on collisions do to automobiles. The damage is always heavy, the repairs are certain to be drastic and costly, and the restored versions, if they can be repaired, will never really be quite as sound as the original.

Yet, while we do everything in our power to avoid crashing our cars, we have always been far more reckless with our relationships. Our society seems to cry more over a crushed car than a mangled marriage.

If his game is right, an athlete can't go wrong admitting to adultery. If the economy is strong, a president can't be weakened by attempting to cover it up.

Can it be that we now give adultery a pass because marriage no longer matters to us? Perhaps the attacks on the family structure have finally induced an insensitivity to infidelity.

If, as a society, we took the sin of adultery more seriously, perhaps we might not consider its only crime to be getting caught.

Frank Turner

Believing the Bible

Finally tonight: believing the Bible and why making that one major decision for myself has made all my other decisions for me.

So many people are unquestionably in a quandary over how to live their lives. The usual standards are usually unstable: right today, wrong tomorrow; abhorrent yesterday, acceptable today; prohibited by one generation and promoted by the next.

But, while makeshift morals are causing social confusion, the laws we originally set to live by are much less ambiguous. From this country's constitution and its document declaring independence, to every canon, edict and decree; statute by statute, they all have their basis in the Bible and what was originally carved in stone by its ultimate author.

It is that kind of rock solid foundation that keeps me from wavering in whatever new age wind is blowing.

My final decisions on everything from Harry Potter to homosexuality, from liquor to lotteries, abortion, *The Bachelor* and casinos—everything from A to Z—can all be found between the book covers from Genesis to Revelation.

It is, for anyone, a big decision; but it's the last decision a Bible believer has to make.

Frank Turner

The Power of Believing

Faith is the most powerful element of our relationship with God. The promise of His salvation is *granted through faith*:

> that if you confess with your mouth the Lord Jesus and believe in your heart that God has raised Him from the dead, you will be saved. For with the heart one believes unto righteousness, and with the mouth confession is made unto salvation (Romans 10:9–10).

The righteousness of Christ is *imputed* (or accounted to us) *by faith.* Concerning Abraham, whom God used to give us an example of righteousness being accounted through faith, the Apostle Paul writes:

> Now it was not written for his sake alone that it was imputed to him, but also for us. It shall be imputed to us who believe in Him who raised up Jesus our Lord from the dead, who was delivered up because of our offenses, and was raised because of our justification (Romans 4:23–25).

Faith is the foundation of our ability to please God and the key that unlocks the blessings of God in our lives.

But without faith *it is* impossible to please *Him,* for he who comes to God must believe that He is, and *that* He is a rewarder of those who diligently seek Him (Hebrews 11:6).

Faith in Christ is the single most important *gift* from God.

"For God so loved the world that He **gave** His only begotten Son, that whoever believes in Him should not perish but have everlasting life. For God did not send His Son into the world to condemn the world, but that the world through Him might be saved" (John 3:16–17, emphasis added by author).

"Nor is there salvation in any other, for there is no other name under heaven **given** among men by which we must be saved." (Acts 4:12, emphasis added by author).

For by grace you have been saved through faith, and that not of yourselves; *it is* the **gift** of God, not of works, lest anyone should boast. (Ephesians 2:8–9, emphasis added by author).

We have so many magnificent and wonderful promises in Christ, and yet not one of them can be apprehended without faith. For instance:

Christ accomplished the payment for our sins at His cross, but you can only accept the promise of that payment by *faith*.

Christ provides the righteousness that is imputed to us from His perfect life, but you can only receive the promise that it is accounted to us by *faith*.

Christ has won our victory over death, hell, and the grave through his resurrection and turned his empty tomb into an open door through which we can step into eternal life, but you can only gain that victory by *faith*.

Christ has provided the Holy Spirit to comfort us, seal us, lead us into all truth, guide us and teach us, but we can only receive the promise of this amazing gift by *faith*.

Faith is the single most powerful and wonderful element of our relationship with God and it is His *gift* to us. Everything God has ever done for man has had the singular purpose of revealing Himself to us to create, foster and strengthen our *faith* in Him.

In John's gospel, which includes the account of Lazarus being raised from the dead, the word *believe* occurs more than eighty times. Indeed, the entire account concerning Lazarus was included for the same reason the Lord performed the miracle of raising him from the dead: that we would *believe*.

Jesus said, "Take away the stone." Martha, the sister of him who was dead, said to Him, "Lord, by this time there is a stench, for he has been dead four days." Jesus said to her, "Did I not say to you that if you would **believe** you would see the glory of God?" Then they took away the stone from the place where the dead man was lying. And Jesus lifted up His eyes and said, "Father, I thank You that You have heard Me. And I know that You always hear Me, but because of the people who are standing by I said this, that they may believe that You sent Me." Now when He had said these things, He cried with a loud voice, "Lazarus, come forth!" And he who had died came out bound hand and foot with graveclothes, and his face was wrapped with a cloth. Jesus said to them, "Loose him, and let him go." Then many of the Jews who had come to Mary, and had seen the things Jesus did, **believed** in Him (John 11:39–45, emphasis added by author).

Dear friends, this is why I have this testimony and why I am sharing it with you: *that you may believe*. The reason I am sharing every deep dark element of my destruction is so that *you will believe* in the one who restored me. The reason I am sharing every detail of my descent into sin is so that *you will believe* in the one who redeemed me. The reason I am sharing every agony of how I received the promised payment of death as the wage of sin is so that *you will believe* in the one who resurrected me.

The only way to salvation is Christ. The Lord says so Himself. He did not merely tell us the truth, He actually *is* the truth. He does not just promise eternal life, He *is* the life. And He did not die on the cross to merely provide a way, He *is* the way.

> Jesus said to him, "I am the way, the truth, and the life. No one comes to the Father except through Me" (John 14:6).

The only way to salvation is to accept Christ. And the only way to accept Christ *is to believe.*

A Final Thought

I laugh out loud when I turn on my radio or television or stumble across a website and see some so-called "theologian" trying to explain why believers in Christ can only hope for two things: Heaven eventually and misery immediately.

Don't be ignorant or misled. I was destroyed. Now I have been restored. I believe Christ for all of His promises and all of His promises toward me are being fulfilled. God responds to faith. It is literally that simple.

When doubters preach that divine health, healing, financial stability and abundance, wisdom, peace, joy, dominion, authority and power are not available to every single born again believer in Christ...well...I will not mince words—they are lying to you.

Break away from the pack of doubters and decide right now to have an *uncommon* relationship with God.

Everything I've written to you in this testimony is so that you will believe God can, and will, do for you everything He did for Lazarus and for me by raising us from the dead; and for millions of others who have just done what most aren't willing to do...believe God.

Life After Death

During the nearly seven years following my return to Channel 7 in 2000, the Lord promoted me again from the weekends to the weeknights and from the small-time to the big show. And for a time, not only was I doing the number one, most watched 5:00 nightly newscast, and the 7:00 nightly newscast with its historic Christian commentaries, but I was also anchoring the 10:00 *Action News* broadcast which ran on the independent station UPN 50.

So the devil managed to destroy me and ruin my career as I did one newscast, but God restored me and returned me to television to do three newscasts on two different channels.

We managed a full-time evangelistic, deliverance and healing ministry, with me preaching in hundreds of churches, primarily on weekends.

After marrying the woman of my dreams in 1999, Nicky and I had the joy of our daughter Allyson (Ally) being born in 2002 and our daughter Rachel in 2004.

On October 9, 2006, I retired from Channel 7 to devote all my time to the preaching of the gospel; and in March of 2007, I was ordained as a pastor.

We are now free to devote all our time to spreading the truth of the Lord Jesus Christ around the world through the building of our international ministry.

Come and hear me preach sometime and meet my family. We love you.

The Turner family, 2005 (*Portraits by Alex*, Brighton MI).

To order additional copies of *Raised from the Dead*, or to find out about other books by Frank Turner, please visit our website at www.frankturner.org.